Random Thoughts as I Age

Things Nobody Told Me

Judy Cline

Random Thoughts as I age

Copyright © 2020 Judy Cline

All rights reserved under International and Pan-American Copyright Conventions.

No portion of this book may be reproduced, distributed or transmitted in any form or by any means including photocopying, recording or other electronic or mechanical means, without the prior written permission of the author, except by a reviewer who may quote brief passages in a review.

Published by ClineWorks, solely owned by Judy Cline

Printed and distributed by IngramSpark

Book and Cover Design by Magnolia Creative
Fort Erie, Ontario, Canada

BISAC BIO 026000, FAM 005000, FAM 021000

Keywords

Aging/surprises/truths/joy/sorrow/lessons/contentment/love

ISBN 978-0-9867398-3-5

*This book dedicated to Wes
who gives me comfort and strength*

Foreword

Welcome to my random thoughts. I had an interesting conversation with my husband about why I wanted to make these thoughts into a book. After lots of introspection I know that it is part vanity, the sheer pleasure of holding another book with my name on it as author. I think a stronger reason is the feedback from friends who have sampled sections and feel these thoughts should be shared.

After reading a few pages a friend told she was moved by what I had written, that she had similar thoughts over the years but could never put them into words. Another felt that I expressed a positive approach to aging with a real life mixture of sad and happy experiences. He described the stories as significant memories with thoughts about how life should be lived and of lessons learned. The best message was you have good ideas and you write well … write more. So, I have written more and here are the random thoughts.

Naming this book was a challenge. I really wanted to call it Nobody Told Me because it described the first thought that helped spawn all the others. Being someone who loves words and composes thoughts into actual sentences (even as I am falling asleep) I wrote many of them down.

As the years have gone by and these thoughts have come I realize how surprising some of them are. Some of the pieces in this book were written recently, some several years ago. They all deal with revelations as I age. I'm sure there still are many things about aging that I don't know – many other things nobody told me.

As to choosing the title, the last book I wrote was appropriately called Never Give Up, the motto of the book's subject, Eleanor Mills. I didn't realize at the time that Never Give Up is the title and/or the subtitle of many, many books currently in print.

This time I wanted to avoid choosing a title that was mirrored many times over by other books. I wanted one that would stand out from the crowd and hopefully intrigue. I realized the obvious title was the one on this cover, Random Thoughts as I Age –Things Nobody Told Me.

Now I realize perhaps somebody did tell me and I didn't listen because I was young and busy. These thoughts would have seemed totally unrelated to me in my youth. As the years have gone by and retrospection has become part of my life, I realized the proper focus for the title is these thoughts that have come to me as I age.

Perhaps you, my readers already know these things. If the thoughts are new to you please let me share them.

The thing about Hair 1

The Happiness Curve 5

On Choosing a Career 9

Media Experiences 15

You can Reinvent Yourself every few years 19

On Writing 25

Clearing your Workspace Improves your Productivity 29

Sometimes Childhood Dreams should stay Dreams 31

One of your Kids fulfills a Secret Dream 35

A Non-athlete gets to Pretend 39

How Lucky to Find the Right Occupation 43

On becoming a Family Physio 45

Random Remarks 51

On Patience 53

On Being a Parent 61

You Cannot Form or Change your Child 65

Raising Kids is the Best Way to Grow up Ourselves 67

The Truth about Being a Grandparent 71

The Instant Kinship when Meeting Cousins 75

On the Death of a Friend 79

You're Never Old Enough to be an Orphan 83

About Dodie 85

The Importance of a Chance to Mourn 89

Being an Only Child is not all it's Cracked up to Be 93

Mourning a Garden 99

Food can Say I Love You 105

Cooking Gets More and More Interesting 107

My Love/Hate Relationship with a Dishwasher 111

Cross-stitched Irony 115

On Vision 119

Which is Worse, to lose Sight or Hearing 121

The Wonders of Engineers and Surgeons recreating Human Joints. 123

The Importance of Light 125

Forever in Blue Jeans 129

The Realities of an Aging Body 133

Degrees of Separation	135
Thoughts on Bucket Lists	137
On Love and How it Changes	141
On Days that Grow Short	145
The Pleasures of Leaving the Snowbird Life	149
Making Friends as we Age	155
How Liberating it is to Buy the last of Many Things	157
On memories of People we Loved	161
Thoughts During a Pandemic	163
On Obituaries	167
On Clearing Out and Ridding Up	171
Entering Stage 2 of a Pandemic	177
Getting a Job at 82	181
I Thought Growing Old would Take Longer	183
The Physio becomes the Patient	185
The Ending to this Unusual Year	187
Afterword	191

Judy Cline

The Thing about Hair

Almost everyone has it. There are a few minor exceptions including bald new born and old people, those having chemo for cancer or someone with alopecia. But aside from these everybody has hair. It comes in many colours, shapes and lengths and can be curly or straight, shiny or dull.

The thing about hair that surprised me is that not everyone has hair that hurts. My hair is rather coarse and used to be almost black, now so white that I'm almost a blonde. It has a decided mind of its own regarding curls and which direction it plans to go at any time. For most of my life, when I wake up my hair has chosen a strange path and it hurts. I thought that was one of those universal things, so universal that nobody ever mentioned it.

One strange weekend many years ago, we drove with friends overnight from St. Catharines to Boston to be spectators at an amazing rowing regatta called The Head of the Charles. We arrived in Boston about 7 a.m., found a restaurant that served us a substantial breakfast of steak, eggs and home fries with pots and pots of coffee. Because our hotel room wouldn't be ready until after 1 p.m., we did a mini-drive and walk tour of Boston. Most of the town seemed asleep so it was a fun tour without much traffic. We even walked through Harvard and visited the Coop with no crowds.

Lack of sleep caught up to us at the hotel, so we all had a nap, perhaps 2 hours. After the nap we gathered into one room and made plans to go tour again then find a lobster house for dinner. I asked to have a chance to shower and wash my hair, as it was hurting. My husband and my best friend laughed at my phrase, my friend's husband agreed with me that he also needed to wash his hurting hair. We were told that it wasn't possible for hair to hurt, and I realized what really hurt was my scalp which was being pulled every which way by the self-directed hair.

Checking my husband and my best friend, we with the hurting hair pronounced that they both had wimpy hair with no will of its own. If your hair doesn't hurt you have weak willed hair, hair that doesn't challenge you. If it does you are being tested and strengthened by your strong willed hair.

Nobody told me that not everybody had hair that hurt.

The Happiness Curve

Steve Paikin had a very interesting Agenda last week. It was, as always meticulously researched and featured two segments, three new books and their authors. The theme was aging. One of the books details a recent study of happiness of populations in many countries. Regardless of the country, the graph of happiness at specific ages is replicated in every one. The high and low points of the curve vary from one country to another, but the shape is essentially the same for each.

The curve begins in childhood with a high level of happiness. The level gradually drops until it reaches its lowest point somewhere between ages 45 and 55. Remarkably it then begins to rise again and continues that rise until age 100. Apparently testing of chimpanzees shows the same curve, although I am still trying to figure out how chimps were tested for happiness.

It was an interesting and comforting study. I do remember when I was over 60 talking to younger friends who held pity parties as they turned 40 then 50. They seemed to be feeling as if they were on a downward slide to old age and decrepitude. I told them then that the best was yet to come. After 60 you had the best of both worlds, you were old enough to do anything you wanted and also old enough to use your age as an excuse to avoid doing things you didn't want to do.

Last evening we had dinner with friends who have just had a year in which one partner was treated for melanoma and the other had heart surgery to insert a stent. The dinner conversation steered toward how we all felt. We spoke of feeling more at peace; more content, happier and we were trying to identify the "why". We are past worrying about losing a job, the children are grown and doing tolerably well. They are no longer our sole focus nor our sole responsibility. Our aspirations are much less and we are content at this time.

Nobody told me how right I was when I said it just got better and better.

> When I was five years old my mother always told me that happiness was the key to life. When I went to school, they asked me what I wanted to be when I grew up. I wrote down "happy". They told me that I didn't understand the assignment. I told them they didn't understand life.
>
> John Lennon

On Choosing a Career

I grew up with two older brothers as the daughter of a manager and a registered nurse. It was an awesome family in many ways. My mother taught my brothers how to cook and my father taught me how to put a new plug on a toaster. I was lucky to be the daughter in a family where girls and boys were treated equally.

My brothers both went to university studying engineering. There was no question that, despite the cost to a family with a modest income, I could and should also go to university. I loved art, mathematics and physics, did cross word and jigsaw puzzles and read mysteries regularly. Architecture sounded alluring, but the 50's were not a good time to enter that field as a woman. I also wondered about engineering despite the fact that in the 1950's only 1% of first year students were female.

From age 11 to 12 I wore an ugly back brace because of a dorsal kyphosis, a possible result of a very rapid growth spurt. I met a physiotherapist who gave me exercises I hated. That must have been subliminally in my mind when I met with the Deans of both Engineering and Physical and Occupational Therapy (P&OT) at the University of Toronto. I was warned that it would be a tough road in Engineering as a woman although there was no doubt that I could handle the academics involved. The Dean of P&OT impressed on me that P&OT was a very challenging occupation, demanding exceptional qualities and skills. Whatever else Dr. Jousse said to me that day, his challenge made me opt for P&OT.

We were known on campus as the Honours Basket Weavers, and yes, that was a very small part of our studies. The course combined many academic studies with hands on learning, supplemented in second and third years with "placements" at various hospitals and centres throughout Toronto. It was a privilege to have been accepted into the program and it was not easy to continue maintaining a good average.

My first job was in the physiotherapy department at the former Nora Frances Henderson Hospital (now Juravinski Hospital) on the Mountain in Hamilton, for the princely sum of $55 week. Although I had been hired as a physio I spent my first four months there as the sole charge occupational therapist. One of the OTs had taken a four-month leave of absence and the other was moving out of the city after her recent marriage.

The hospital was a general hospital with a varied caseload, which included a small psychiatric ward. I had patients with anxiety neuroses, ones with severe low back pain, with strokes and amputations, various neurologic conditions and the aftermath of polio all referred to me. It was overwhelming at times, I was 20 years old and there was no other OT with whom to discuss patient treatment plans.

The charge physiotherapist who had hired me had been my supervisor the previous summer when I did my mandatory two-month internship there. She was a wise and wonderful woman, recognizing my struggles and convincing me that sometimes good enough was actually, good enough. She taught me to do the best I could with each situation then go home wiping my mind of the day's worries. There was time enough the next morning to begin again to make someone else's life better and richer. This was a valuable lesson learned very early in my career.

I was grateful to move back to the physiotherapy side after four months. It was a great learning environment with a supervisor who praised and taught as she praised. I moved into private practice in Hamilton, at a clinic owned by an orthopaedic surgeon for a brief period. Working there I began to realize how much my interest in physics, in puzzles and their solutions fit with doing orthopaedic physiotherapy.

I managed three pregnancies interspersed with short working sessions. When my mentor and guru left the hospital to establish a private facility that had no connection to any hospital, an unusual concept then, she hired me. It was an exciting place to work, sharing with other therapists and treating what we called the walking wounded.

Barbara continued to teach me how to reach for better and better outcomes for my patients (now of course they're called clients). I could discuss a treatment or a problem with her, she would compliment me on the good things that I had done and then quietly add a suggestion about something that would enhance that treatment. It was a wonderful way to make me stretch and gently correct without ever making me feel diminished. I think I would have tried to walk on water, if she had asked.

Nobody told me how perfect a fit physiotherapy would be for many of my interests and talents

Media Experiences

I did love, do love, and always will, love words. I also was for many years and in my heart still am, a physiotherapist. I was able to combine the love of words by speaking and writing through my active years as a physiotherapist.

I often spoke to community groups about various topics relating to physical health and safety. Other than an occasional bottle of wine, it was unpaid. The speaking was a thank you for the opportunity I had been given by my family and by the university to train for that perfect for me profession. I know that I did pay tuition, books and living expenses with a lot of help and sacrifice from my parents. I also know that the actual cost of the tuition was much in excess of the bill we paid. The community talks were a small way to say thanks.

I usually prepared a small handout for each speech, hoping that I could write clearly enough to reinforce my message. From those simple handouts, more writing grew. I was asked to write articles for publication in our local newspaper, then in some health journals and for group newsletters. It was fun, I found the writing fairly straightforward to do and occasionally I would hear from someone who had read what I had written.

From the writing came some very interesting opportunities. I appeared on two TV programs, speaking as a movement specialist on gardening safety. One of the programs was a live morning show from CTV in Toronto. Apparently I did well, although I never saw a video of the program as none of my friends who watched the show taped it. Perhaps that was a good thing as the actuality of our appearance often can be shockingly different from the one we see in our minds. Appearing on the show was not nearly as scary as driving to the other side of Toronto early on a weekday morning to appear on the show. The other show was taped, so much easier on the whole.

I did several radio interviews, both locally and further away. The very best one was on CFRB in Toronto on a call-in show. I had always wondered why the experts on such shows were able to come up with good answers so quickly. Sitting in the studio with the host and another physio, we were able to see a screen showing the callers' questions. There was a two to three minute delay before the caller's voice appeared on the monitor giving us time to form an answer. Perhaps the best part was being able to simply ignore a question that was argumentative or likely to need a 20-minute answer. Now I understand why radio hosts feel so powerful.

Nobody told me that these delightful opportunities would present themselves.

You can Reinvent Yourself Every Few Years

I remember an article in McLeans magazine many years ago, featuring an interview with a dentist in his early fifties, discussing his life and his dreams. Paraphrasing his quotes, he said, my life has been okay. I am a good dentist and have been able to provide a fine life for my family and myself. However, I am bored with my work. Too much of it is repetitive. The challenge for the most part is long gone. I am asking myself at this stage in my life what right did the 19 year old me have to decide the direction of the next 30 years of my life? I really want to do something else, something that will excite and stimulate me, that will stretch my abilities and make me yearn to get up and regret having to sleep. At this time in my life I am bored and unhappy.

That was interesting reading at the time. As I remember it now, I know that he really didn't have to be a dentist forever. It would have been difficult to become say a pilot or the president of a large corporation at that stage of his life but change was possible.

My choice to study Physical and Occupational Therapy was a good one. I love to be around people and knew I didn't want to work in isolation. Physiotherapy let me work with people and ultimately as I moved more and more into orthopaedic physiotherapy I could use my love of logic and physics in my work. The laws of physics apply equally to the human body as to the inanimate world. A lever is a lever is a lever.

I had a satisfying and challenging career in physiotherapy, working first in institutions but ultimately in private practice. The private world was more challenging, as it involved no government funding, while giving me freedom to put my patient/clients needs first. My best patients were probably the self-employed as they, like me, knew how hard and well you had to work to ensure that eventually there was a buck that stopped in your own pocket.

I began to feel, as did that dentist did so long ago that there were parts of me not being used, that there were things I still needed to do and things I wanted to try. Never would I describe it as a "bucket list" as that implies a feeling of urgency to fulfill unfilled hopes and dreams. It was much more thoughts of what talents did I have that were unused and what parts of my brain needed to be awakened.

I discovered an entrepreneur inside me and branched into some side businesses, including finding well-made and inexpensive braces and supports for my clients. When computers were new and being dropped onto almost every executive's desk I decided to learn how to modify work areas to reduce the aches and pains related to their use. It might have been okay to keep treating them for those injuries, but it made more sense to figure out how to fix the cause. The human body is very flexible and adjustable and people can go through strange contortions to adjust to a physical environment. I worked hard teaching people how to move their workstations around, adapting the station to the body instead of adapting the body to the station.

When I was planning to retire I wanted something to engross and engage me as much in retirement as physiotherapy had. I wanted to retire to something, not just from something. There was a side of me that played at creativity. I painted and drew, but destroyed many of the paintings, as what I saw in my head didn't seem to come out my fingertips. My paternal grandmother had run a florist business and I had learned some techniques from her. I tried making arrangements of dried or silk flowers, but discovered the competition at craft fairs was huge in the floral arts.

I sewed for fun and for economy, and loved playing with colour and design. For several years after retirement I entered juried craft and art shows and usually sold just enough to buy new supplies. The problem with these creative activities was when a new design or article sold well I didn't want to replicate it over and over. It was much more interesting to design something new. It also became more difficult to compete with inexpensive so-called handcrafted items available through chain and dollar stores.

I had written several manuals relating to my physiotherapy work. I also wrote articles on various physio related topics for a local newspaper. In my 70's I began to write more seriously. I wrote descriptions of social activities and seminars that happened in the community to which we moved in 2013. I now get writing assignments from the editor of the monthly newsmagazine. It's pretty exciting as most get printed with my by-line! I have written more manuals, one with practical advice for anyone having hip or knee replacement surgery. I have just published my first real book, the biography of a gutsy and amazing woman in her late 70's, badly bent over because of severe osteoporosis.

The excellent teacher I had in Grade Thirteen English would be delighted. He was disappointed that I chose a practical course at university instead of going for an Honours BA majoring in English. So would my college roommate who had told me many years ago that I should write. I feel as if I have reinvented myself several times over. In this latest incarnation I can't wait to sit down at my computer and write.

Nobody told me how many times I could reinvent myself and becoming a writer would be the latest one.

On Writing

I have joined a small informal writers' group. I've attended three times to date and it is very interesting to sit and talk with others who are also in love with words. Apparently I carry a certain cachet since I have written and actually published one book. I was asked at the first meeting if I would talk about the process of writing. That was a humbling request.

That first book was a project I felt compelled to write. It tells the story of Eleanor Mills, who in her 70s inspired a walk in 130 communities across Canada to tell others about the horrors of osteoporosis. No one had told her story and I was afraid no one ever would.

Perhaps all writers write from compulsion. Certainly some of the best Canadian writers do. I have a wondrous book compiled by the daughter and grandson of Carol Shields, titled *Startle and Illuminate.* Apparently, as well as being a sublime writer Carol was also a mentor to many writers. I am not sure that I will ever achieve writing that startles and illuminates, but I hope that someday, something I write may manage one or the other.

I naively thought the writing of Eleanor's story would take 12 to 18 months, that I would find someone who wanted to publish it and the task would be done. The writing took four years and I found publishers aren't interested in brand new writers of biographies. I discovered that even Terry Fallis self published his first book, *The Best Laid Plans.* He found an established publisher for new editions of that book and his subsequent books once he had received critical acclaim and awards for the first one.

Researching self-publishing options was a job within the job. There are many companies providing a variety of services, for very similar prices. I spent time reading their promotional literature, talking to representatives, wondering which of the many services offered did I want and or need. Did I want to publish in soft cover or hard cover, were there enough people who had embraced e-readers to add that format? Did I want to retain full editorial control over what I wrote or let the company do more of the work in exchange for a smaller return to me on each sale? I finally made a decision and sent the first instalment.

Thinking back, the price was not exorbitant. I had wondered if the design service was something I could do myself. I'm glad I didn't try. Taking the manuscript, separating the chapters, numbering them (which I still have trouble doing), adding chapter titles and a proper index, inserting the photos, which I had scanned and sent separately, and generally making it look pretty was what the company did as part of their design service.

For the base price I got three free revisions. I was not as careful as I should have been and had to pay for a further revision when I realized that I had reversed names for two people in several of the photos. I consoled myself that at least I had made the mistake consistently throughout the book.

I made a rough design for the cover, which the company improved. I made many decisions including, pricing, discounts for booksellers and accepting returns decisions made easier with advice from the company.

Then I began the process of telling the world about this, to my mind, wonderful story of an amazing woman. I tried to market myself as a storyteller, talking about Eleanor and the book hoping that I could recoup some of my costs while sharing her story. I did not know how long it would take, how much work there was still to do after it was written and how satisfying all the time and cost would prove to be.

Nobody told me how great it would be to hold a real book I had written in my hands.

Clearing your Workspace Improves your Productivity

I usually have several projects underway and sitting on my desk area at any time. I am paying bills, researching products or projects, answering e-mails and writing. The other area of my workplace where my sewing, crocheting and knitting project materials are is thankfully out of sight when I am at my desk but too apparent when I turn.

Spending twenty minutes filing, sorting and consigning junk to the appropriate wastebasket can improve the work output at my desk amazingly. Empty spots on the horizontal surface inspire me. Stray papers that find the proper home make each of the tasks easier.

Clearing the other work area is usually more complex. At the moment there is a wonderful collection of pillowcases from several thrift shops that will become dresses for little girls. There are two wall hangings of fabric and yarn that are finished except for the backing and hanging loops. Another is waiting until I decide if I will use more paint and machine embroidery with less fabric appliqué to achieve the effect that my mind sees. There is a small pile of ironing and two small bits of mending.

I cleared my desk yesterday and writing today has been easy and has gone well. Tomorrow I will do the little bits of ironing, the two small mending jobs and then make tidy piles of the other projects so that their physical presence is neater and therefore less intimidating. That will set me up for more progress.

Nobody told me clearing your desk clears your mind.

Sometimes Childhood Dreams should stay Dreams

I was the third and last child in my family, with my mother referring to me as "the baby" into my teens! We were neither rich nor poor, part of the great middle class. Nobody in most families then played any organized sports. There were corner lots for marbles, and kick the can and pick up baseball games. In winter there were hills for toboggans and sleds and outdoor skating rinks, usually in back or side yards.

The rinks were made by stomping down snow, attaching the garden hose to a tap in the basement before running it out a cellar window. Every night a father or older brother would stand there spraying down the snow and building up an ice surface. As adults, the one we made in our backyard had an interesting wrinkle. It ran with a slight slope from south to north, making it an easy place to learn how to skate backwards.

As a child I wore whatever skates one of my brothers had just outgrown. They were, of course tube skates, brown leather with black toecaps. One year as a special treat my mother bought me a used pair of white tube skates. The first time I laced them on I was impressed with the look of girl skates on my feet. They were no different to skate with than the brown/black combo I had been using but they looked so much better.

Fairly early in our marriage my husband gave me a pair of brand new white figure skates! I was impressed and delighted with this wonderful gift. I pictured myself moving gracefully around the rink, perhaps even managing to skate in modest circles. I was excited about wearing them, cradling them in the box until we got to a real rink.

They of course had picks on the toes. Now anyone who has learned to skate with tube skates can come close to killing themselves with figure skates. The forward motion with a tube skate drives the bottom pick on figure skates right into the ice, usually propelling the skater onto her nose. I avoided ruining my nose that way but had numerous bruises on my knees and hips from falls.

I got some instruction from a friend who had grown up with figure skates. I asked the skate sharpener to remove the bottom pick. Neither the pick removal nor the advice helped me at all. Eventually I had all the picks ground off and went back to my old style of skating. I kept those skates, and remembered the joy of getting real women's skates until one of my sons outgrew his hockey skates. I retired the white skates and happily skated in the new, old hand me downs.

Nobody told me I was better off just dreaming about real white women's skates.

One of your Kids Fulfills a Secret Dream

My life has taken some surprising twists. Most of them have turned out to be interesting, satisfying or just plain fun. Maybe the black Scot in my heritage felt planning too much would be tempting fate. However there was an activity I had always secretly hoped to do. I never mentioned it because living in Southern Ontario, where winter ping pongs from cold and snowy to messy melt I knew it couldn't happen. Perhaps reading Jack London in my youth put the thought there. I pictured travelling by dog sled, behind a team of dogs with pointy, radar ears and strong, lithe bodies. This wasn't going to happen in the Niagara/Hamilton area.

Our first-born son went to Lakehead University in Thunder Bay. He met and married a local girl and has lived there since his early twenties. We visit them as often as we can both in winter and in summer. One winter visit he announced we had a surprise date Sunday afternoon and had to leave the house by 11 am. The drive was pretty with lots of snow in the bush but none on the roads. We turned off at a picture showing a team of sled dogs. As we drove into a clearing there were several dog houses, each with a dog either beside or in it. I was excited hoping that we could meet some of the dogs. The surprise was that he had booked an excursion for us.

As the owners came out with two sleds and traces every dog came to attention, barking with excitement. They all seemed to be shouting "pick me" eager to be part of the teams. He and his wife hooked up the two teams. The dogs not chosen stood there with drooping tails and lowered heads.

The trip was as sleek and fast as my dreams. The dogs seemed to move with little effort, grabbing mouthfuls of snow as they ran. Each team had a leader, chosen for both temperament and staying ability. We travelled along a trail in light bush and stopped at a cabin on the edge of a frozen lake. We went inside and over hot chocolate saw pictures and heard stories of several iditarods the owner had been in.

During these competitions the precautions taken to keep the dogs safe are impressive. At every stop a veterinarian inspects each dog. A dog judged to be unhealthy to continue has a large mark spray painted onto his/her back to ensure they don't continue to race. Apparently the dogs feel the shame of going home by truck and mope all the way.

The dogs were an interesting mixture of colours, many of them with that clear, light blue husky eye. Three of the dogs looked as if they had some Golden Retriever mixed with husky. Apparently a wandering male had come by, impregnating one of the Husky females. She had six pups, three of them being kept by the owners. They told us they regretted letting the other three go as the ones they kept exhibited the stamina of the Husky with the incredible willingness to please of the Golden.

The trip was a joy and a great way to spend a cold snowy afternoon. On our way back to the house I told my son that I had always had this secret wish. He had, unknowingly fulfilled it for me.

Nobody told me my son was a mind reader.

A Non-Athlete gets to Pretend

I was a tomboy growing up, with two older brothers. There was vacant land in the neighbourhood where we would play tag, hide and seek, kick the can and 21 or move-up baseball. My parents were tall, my dad a seriously good athlete in his teens. I grew tall as well, much of it in a very short period when I was eleven leaving me with the affliction of many fast growing kids. For most of my youth I was never sure where the ends of my arms and legs were. When we played pickup baseball with the neighbouring kids I was usually allowed five tries at bat before I was retired. Since I don't recall ever connecting the bat to the ball, I might as well have been given two or twenty tries.

In high school I participated in the usual Physical Education activities of gymnastics (couldn't manage a head stand or a cartwheel), volleyball, basketball and various track activities without wowing anyone with my prowess. I did try out for the junior basketball team and was the last cut. I think the coach had been hoping until the end I might be able to add some skills in passing, dribbling or shooting to the height advantage I had. My total lack of hand eye co-ordination disappointed him more than it did me.

Math classes were fun as was English. I participated in the debating club, played a cornet in the Concert band and was involved in the drama club as a makeup person, sewer of costumes and a bit part actor. Athletics never tempted me.

Moving forward through university, marriage, motherhood there were no sports in my life. The most physical I got was in a garden or helping with house projects. I got good at toe nailing studs and holding up sheets of plasterboard for someone else to attach to the ceiling! I actually won a nail-hammering contest at a company picnic with my three kids cheering me on. There was still nothing approaching skill in athletics through this period.

I trained and worked as a physiotherapist. After moving to St. Catharines my husband and I became involved in the rowing community. I volunteered with the weigh in crew and was involved in setting up a first aid presence on the island during regattas. I also began to work with some of the coaches when an athlete experienced physical problems. I was able to go out in a coach boat with one of the national team coaches and study the movements a rower made. It is very hard to analyze the motions involved in rowing on land but great to be on the water with a coach watching the full cycle.

Being a long time fan of both puzzles and physics my physio practice gravitated toward solving orthopaedic problems. Working with rowers offered interesting problems to solve, the rowers being anxious and keen to do what they could to get back on the water and perform well.

Out of this volunteer work, I was given a chance to travel with athletes from the St. Catharines Clubs to out of town regattas, then to time trials for the Canadian Row-

body, to understand what I found on examination, how the findings related to their presenting problem and how I planned to resolve that problem. The next challenge was to give them the tools to manage themselves. There have been many times when I met a former patient at a social event, often years later, who would proudly tell me they still remembered what I taught them to do if there was a recurrence.

What a gift I was given to end up in a profession where my talents and interests allowed me to be successful.

Nobody told me how much satisfaction there would be in becoming a physiotherapist.

> *To love what you do and feel that it matters – how could anything be more fun?*
>
> *Katherine Graham*

On Becoming A Family Physio

When we moved to St. Catharines, there were literally no jobs in physiotherapy. In the past, there were so many openings that a therapist would often fill out the application form for the job during a break on the first day of work. My husband was busy at a new, interesting job. The kids were all in school and active with both day and after school activities. I was thoroughly bored. I even resorted to reading romance novels, a pastime that lasted two days and four novels.

Finally I found a maternity leave fill in for six months, working half days at the Hotel Dieu Hospital in the physiotherapy department. In some ways it was a continuation of the type of patients I was accustomed to seeing as we treated a fair number of outpatients. We also brought patients down from the wards for treatment. The Dieu was a full service hospital, except for maternity, so the caseload was varied.

I found myself becoming frustrated by the seeming need to maintain a waiting list to ensure that we kept the full staff complement. I often felt that longer initial assessments and longer time spent teaching prevention would decrease the number of visits each patient needed, thereby decreasing the wait list.

The maternity leave ended and I worked with the Niagara Home Care Program. This job let me use my OT as well as my PT side. It was a luxury to have one patient at a time seeing them in their own home and being able to interact with their families. You could educate your patient how to safely get into and out of the shower, you could move furniture around to enable them to walk safely and you could help re-organize a kitchen for easier cooking and clean-up. Exercises were practical things, using tin cans and sugar bags for resistance and teaching someone to stand up twice every time they stood as an easy way to strengthen legs.

However, my entrepreneurial side was calling to me. I

wanted to work in an outpatient facility that gave me freedom to set my own timings with patients, where the paperwork had only the most important information and every treatment included a large element of education. The combination of puzzles and physics continued to intrigue me.

Eventually, as my kids grew I began my own private practice, first with a partner and then solo. It was a challenge as there was no public funding for out of hospital physiotherapy. Patients needed to either have generous health care benefits or be willing to pay personally for their treatment.

Regular courses led me to new ways of thinking. Manual therapy courses became available and they offered excellent ways of assessing. Many more good mentors entered my life, teaching me how to question and perhaps most important to listen. One of my instructors would say, "listen to the patient long enough and quietly enough and they'll tell you what's wrong."

Although medical referral was a requirement for most patients claiming through a health benefit plan, my referrals came most often from other current patients. My receptionist would chuckle sometimes when a request would come from someone new, citing a friend or relative as the referring source.

My practice was varied, young and old, male and female and mostly orthopaedic. I treated mothers and fathers, who brought in their young soccer playing kids. I volunteered at regattas in the first aid area and learned about the demands of rowing and how to get young athletes safely back in a racing shell.

In time young women whose knees I had treated in their teens came to me with sore necks or wrists from their jobs after graduation, often sharing their wedding plans with me. I might see them again during their first pregnancies with back pain. And later, I would sometimes get to check out the strained ankle of that child.

I treated whole families in my years of practice, granddads, fathers, children, sisters and aunts. Made me think of the G&S words "and so did their sisters and their cousins and their aunts." Several people began to refer to me as their family physio, just as they referred to their family dentist or family doctor.

I have been invited to showers, birthday, anniversary and retirement parties. Most recently I attended a memorial service for a dear gentleman, an ex-patient, who had died at 97.

Nobody told me that there was such a category as family physio.

Random Remarks

It is interesting how what seems to be a random remark made a long time ago has an effect that can surprise you. My occupation as a physiotherapist meant that I interacted daily with people, often in pain and feeling emotional distress that went with the physical pain. I learned from several masters of my profession that adding artful listening to skilled physical examinations could assist me in solving the why of presenting pain and disability. My practice began in a typical hospital setting, with a move to private practice first as an employee in another therapist's clinic and then in my own.

I learned to sit quietly during the first assessment visit, asking why the client had come. Some small remarks from me, some 'hmms" and "I sees" would often elicit clear and useful information that would allow me to identify the culprit not the victim. Treating the pain or disability (the victim) was important but long-term good results were achieved by identifying the underlying cause (the culprit). I wanted to be so good at fixing the culprit that the only time I would see the patient would be out in the community or at a gathering, never again in my clinic.

Physiotherapy involves touching and touching opens people's mouths. I would hear about emotional problems, the fatigue of motherhood or the frustration of a dead end job. I never offered counsel on these situations other than suggesting that bodies and hearts can heal, that children do grow, that fatigue can lessen or perhaps that there were other ways to make a living.

Several times when I met a former patient months or years later I was reminded of what one of those random comments, made to comfort, had meant to that person over the years. I think sometimes that our hearts know what remark to make and rarely make the wrong one.

Nobody told me that sometimes the greatest good I had done for a patient was a random remark.

On Patience

Learning patience is such a hard thing to do. One of my favourite signs from many years ago is "Lord, give me patience ... and I want it now!" Even in my 80's there are still times when I want things, including patience, NOW.

As a child, time is very immediate and waiting can be so very difficult. As we get older it can be easier. I've always thought that the length of time we have lived is our measure of time in the present. As a child under ten, summers lasted for months and months. As we get older they shorten, making me think that if my past can be measured in weeks and months, then weeks and months are longer. Once our past begins to be measured in years, then weeks and months pass more quickly. Lately the years seem to be moving very rapidly.

As children we learn patience when we ask a parent for a treat, or their time or a book read and the answer comes, "not yet, but soon." Soon needs to be measured in minutes when we are very young. Soon can be an hour or a day, a week or a year as we mature.

The next lesson in patience must be when you become a parent. The first months, while the baby is picked up, fed, changed, put down aren't too bad as the parent can mostly control the timing. Once independence begins, watching a child struggle to put on a t-shirt the right way or figure out which foot and shoe match can demand a lot of patient "watch and wait" from the parent. The alternative of course is taking over, thus delaying the child's independence. If the ultimate goal of parenting is raising a healthy child to an adulthood of freedom and self-sustenance, then patience as a parent in those early years can be a tough but rewarding thing.

The ultimate lesson in patience, I feel is gardening. I probably started to garden when I was four or five. My paternal grandparents lived in a house that was next to ours on Hamilton Mountain. (No comments from those of you living in vertical mountain ranges. Our Mountain was always referred to as The Mountain and although it only averages 100 m in height it is 725 km long in the Ontario portion alone). My grandfather was a pattern maker by trade, but he and my grandmother owned a good-sized garden plot and had a greenhouse. My grandmother was a florist. I remember helping her make funeral wreaths and picking violets to make posies for her and for my mother.

My Dad moved around southern Ontario with his job as a manager for Central Mortgage and Housing. He puttered (his word) in gardens at each house, loving the long growing seasons in both Windsor and St. Catharines, two of his postings. On his way to work in June he always would tuck a single Paul Scarlet rose into his buttonhole.

I know that my brothers and I puttered with him, starting by planting radishes, a child's delight as the seed germinates so quickly. My eldest brother continued his interest in growing things but after he moved to BC his interest seemed to be in larger plants including fruit trees and the monstrous west coast conifers.

I still have in my small garden here a flowering almond that came from one in my St. Catharines garden. I can trace its genealogy back through our Hamilton garden, to my father's gardens in Kitchener, St. Catharines and Windsor then back to Hamilton and his mother's garden. That plant has yielded little offshoots to the gardens of many friends.

Perennials are perhaps my personal garden favourites. So, getting back to lessons in patience they are the ultimate teachers. They come up each spring (or should)! Depending upon the heat/cold and rain/drought to which they are subjected they may thrive and bloom gorgeously. If the June thunderstorms occur during the week that the peonies are in full bloom, that glory is lost until the next June. The soil can be just what they want; moisture optimal and the sun exposure perfect but the external factors that are beyond our control decide their show that year.

My spring ritual, for every garden I have ever had is a daily stroll watching for the first signs of plant growth. Waiting to see that first delicious sprig of green is to watch renewal. I have a neighbour who still marvels each year as the plants that died last fall rejuvenate themselves. He has gardened for many years, but basically showy annuals such as petunias and marigolds as well as practical crops of tomatoes and raspberries. It's fun to watch his reactions to the glory of perennials.

I applaud the new growth; avoid cultivating early, as I can never quite remember where the lilies and the hostas are planted. I don't think I ever drew up a garden plan, with neat little circles and dots with plants named. I let things grow, ask them if they are content where they are and move them if they're not. I also believe in letting plants self seed or migrate. Periwinkle (vinca minor) is a delight under big old trees but needs to be disciplined annually or more often. Forget-me-nots will carpet the garden with a cloud of blue if you let them. For clean up, just pull the plants after bloom, shake the seed off and let everyone else have a chance at light.

So if this year is a perfect one for my Japanese Tree Peony, I am happy. If it wants to sulk, or bloom in two days only because of an early heat wave I can do nothing except be grateful for the short-term show and wait for next year. Gardening does teach grace and understanding that for everything there is a season and I cannot, no matter how hard I try rush or change or control it.

My latest patience learning experience was writing the story of Eleanor Mills and her cross Canada trek. I found some very early notes recently, with my estimate of time to write and prepare for publication being 12 to 18 months. The reality was four years!

The research, the search for those who were part of the planning and the walk, the identification of pictures and places took such a long time. I learned many new skills chasing sources, copying pictures, verifying quotes and how to actually prepare a book for publication. There's been a lot of hurry up and wait in the process but what I learned as a gardener did help me.

I'm not sure what the next lessons in patience will be, but I'm sure there still are one or two waiting for me.

Nobody told me my long journey of learning patience would never end.

On Being a Parent

BP – before becoming a parent, I had the silly idea that you could have a baby, raise that child to adulthood and then sort of stand back, hopefully admiring your work and their life, then get on with other things.

Sometimes I feel as if the umbilical cords were not so much cut as stretched. I have three children and a borrowed one who has also become mine. They are all close to or over 50 now and managing their own families, careers and lives quite nicely. I have a full and busy life, lots of things to do and enjoy. I talk to them often, love texting and e-mail but generally we live separate lives. However, when one of them has problems with work or has a troubled child I want to leap in and fix things. I still hate to see one of them sad or worried and continue to believe I can somehow make their world wonderful again.

When all of our three had their first babies in the same year, I was reluctant to offer any advice. I think I had bruises on my tongue from biting it. The three are so different, despite the same gene pool and environment growing up. Then, with marriage the dynamics changed again because their spouses (want so badly to say spice) are also so different. Apparently my silence was so marked that my daughter said, "Mom, you can give us advice, we can decide whether to take it."

I still tried to do nothing but approve and cuddle the babies. It seems to have worked as I have good relationships, on the whole, with the in-laws. As those babies grew, I would occasionally make soothing noises about normal behaviour patterns that they went through. Not all the time, but often enough to hopefully reassure the parents.

However when one of my three or four has a crisis, be it emotional or physical all my senses go on alert and I want to ride in and fix. It's really hard to hold a grown child on your lap and rock him or her, especially if the child is over six feet. So I have learned how to use words and food to do the same thing.

I remember a little story from many years ago, when a woman was asked which of her children was her favourite. What a dreadful question to ask! The answer was (names made up of course).... Jane because she is such a good cook, John because he makes me laugh, Peter because he can fix anything and Paul because he is a peacemaker. However, she added, whoever needs me the most at this moment.

That answer is so perfect. Whoever needs me most is the one I love the most just now. Because sometimes the only thing I can give them in their adulthood is the message that I have loved, do love and will love them forever. And of course, although I don't want to wish a crisis on any of them, I really do want to be needed now and again.

Nobody told me that being a parent is forever.

You Cannot Form or Change your Child

Becoming a parent is a wondrous, exciting and scary thing. The many notions that you have before actual parenting begins get shot down very quickly. I used to look at children tearing around with drippy noses and thought how disgusting it was that the mother or father would permit that. Then, eventually as the mother of three, none of whom learned properly how to blow until they were 5 or 6, I felt remorse at my earlier thoughts. It may have been sooner but I began to realize how hard it was to just keep kids fed and safe, let alone clean nosed.

It surprised me to discover the phrases that my mother had used to admonish and educate me while I was growing up would flow out of my mouth so easily. These were the phrases I swore I would never, ever and ever in my life utter.

I also used to feel that I would be able to gently shape my children's lives so that they would be capable of happiness and success in this world. I planned to study their strengths so that I could help enhance those. I would identify their areas of weakness and teach them how to overcome those.

How incredibly naive I was. I realized that no matter what, there was much inborn in each of them. They are all the product of the same mixture of genes. They were raised in the same household with the same parents and as much as possible they were given the same framework of rules and love. They are of course very different, just as their position in the family relating to their siblings is different.

I think along the way I realized that the best I could do for each of them was to recognize their strengths, to applaud their successes and help them deal with their disappointments. I now hope that they each can achieve three things – to love, to be loved and to be responsible. That's still a lot to ask but it would be sufficient.

Nobody told me what I would learn as my children grew.

Raising Kids is the Best Way to Grow up Ourselves

Being a parent has been a really good and fun thing to do. It hasn't always been easy and I'm sure there were times when my parenting skills fell well short of the optimum. There've been many nights of introspection when everyone was in bed wondering if I had truly known when to speak and when to hold my tongue.

I was looking at our wedding picture the other day and marvelling at those two kids (we were 21 and 23 but look absurdly young in the picture) who were so ready to take on the world. We had a couple of years together before we became parents. I remember the awe of holding our firstborn, accompanied by panic, as despite lots of babysitting I had never held a newborn. He is turning out surprisingly well considering the inexperience of his parents. We got better with the next two, and if we'd had more we would have been quite brilliant at the parenting thing.

The other thing we got better at as we continued to parent is growing up ourselves. The sense of responsibility when a child is born to you is amazing. You look at this wonderful baby in your arms, a product of the love you share. You realize that he is totally dependent upon you for food, shelter, warmth and comfort. It is a sobering thought.

Lots of couples now seem to start their families with a pet, sort of practice for the responsibility of having a child. It's not a bad start but the consequences of neglect of a human are a lot greater than of an animal, no matter how beloved.

So to my children, it's been a great ride. I have watched you grow physically, mentally and emotionally. You have become parents and that act of becoming a parent was your final maturing as my parenting you was my final maturing. Now I just get to sit back, love your children and enjoy the view.

Nobody told me how much fun this part of parenting was going to be.

> You grow up the day you have your first real laugh – at yourself
>
> Edith Barrymore

The Truth about Being a Grandparent

Before the first of our grandchildren was born, a dear friend raved about how wonderful it was to be a grandmother. I love her dearly, but thought to myself – sure, sure – babies. I did enjoy our kids as babies, but found them much more interesting as they grew, learning to speak and interact. Watching them learn skills and become independent was a delight. Why was it going to be something special to have a grandchild? I'd been there, done the baby thing and was into a new phase of my life.

Those thoughts stayed with me until I held the first beloved child of my beloved child. The absolute wonder of it floored me. Knowing that this child was the continuation of my husband and me, of our histories, the continuation of my daughter, her husband and his family as well was part of it. The amazing smell of a baby, the remembered scent of powder, milk and warmth was awesome. The tiny hand curled around my finger with startling strength and I was totally hooked.

It has been a joy to cuddle several of these wonders. Watching over them and watching them grow, learn and expand their worlds has been just as big a delight.

I disagree with those who say the best thing about having grandchildren is that you can give them back. The best thing is that you are distanced from the need to ensure enough income to house them and feed them. You don't have the daily routines of getting them up, dressed, off to school or other activities. You now know that much of what each child is and will be is inherent in them. A long-range view, time and distance makes you more optimistic than when you were in the midst of each hour and each day and each crisis. You know that today's crisis does not mean a future disaster.

As grandparents we only have to love them, applaud their triumphs and wipe their tears (sometimes doing the same thing along the way for their parents). Our first grandchildren are now in their 20's beginning to be the adults they are destined to be. I hope that the love we have shared along the way with them have helped that journey.

Nobody told me the real wonder of being a grandparent was the pure love involved.

The Instant Kinship when Meeting Cousins

Several years ago one of my second cousins decided it was time that she got all her cousins together. My brothers and I joined her and her first cousins, along with a cousin (maybe a second or maybe a removed) whose relationship I can only sort out by doing the genealogy. Everybody brought their spouse, so we had kin, in-laws and out-laws. The family we shared came from my paternal grandfather and his siblings, all Christies.

We were to be hosted in Huntsville at my cousin's home on Fairy Lake at her winterized cottage and the smaller one beside. Overflow would be provided at the resort next door and with friendly neighbours. The plan was for everyone to arrive for dinner Monday, with all possibly staying until Friday – the logistics were complex.

People came from British Columbia, Oakville and St. Catharines in Canada and Maryland, New Hampshire and Vermont in the United States.

I know that there was some hesitation on my part and that of my two brothers. I was a little unsure because it had been decades since I had last seen two of the more distant cousins and I didn't remember ever meeting the other one. I expect that our respective spouses felt even more apprehension. One of my brothers was working on a family history and was eager to meet the unknown cousin to help fill in some gaps. He was not really looking forward to the rest of the experience.

It took, perhaps 30 minutes for the strangeness to pass and the conversation to begin. We all talked. We talked to each other and over each other, we told stories of our pasts and remembered stories our parents had shared. I was the youngest of the Christies present and was chosen to make the toast to our parents and grandparents, saying how delighted they would be to know that we had gathered together.

The next day, to decrease the confusion of which Christie was being referenced, my older brother split us into groups as descendants of each line. That helped a bit but we still talked and talked, shared old photos and I heard one of the spouses say, "how can anyone hear or understand when you are all talking". That passion for talk certainly seemed to be the strongest shared characteristic.

It was a wonderful experience and amazing to note the particular tastes and passions that were shared amongst all of us. We shared ancestors but nothing else in the way of occupation, home setting nor even, at this stage citizenship. We collectively had never really spent time together. By Friday, when we really did have to start journeying home – a long drive for many - we had trouble stopping talking and more trouble saying goodbye.

That first gathering was so successful that we have repeated it several times both back in Huntsville and in St. Catharines. Another cousin and his wife joined us at one reunion, travelling from California.

We have visited all the newfound cousin/friends in Maryland, Vermont and New Hampshire. We managed to read and comment on several books, setting up an on-line book club. We still catch up by phone or e-mail on a semi regular basis. We compare gardens, the exploits and trials of our children, whatever we are currently reading and of course, since we all began as Canadians .... the weather.

Nobody told me how great it would be to meet kin and instantly recognize the kinship.

On the Death of a Friend

We were playing at snowbirds in Florida several years ago and had just arrived at a new RV park. I was visiting a recreation hall full of women who were quilting beautiful things. Someone from the office came to give me a message to call our 55-year-old son, at home with his family in Thunder Bay, Ontario. The message was simple, please call - family is okay.

I called and he passed on the sad news that a friend of mine for over 40 years had died unexpectedly. He had some details and told me he had anguished over whether to call to tell me or wait until we came home a month later.

I felt then and still do that he made the right decision. There was to be a brief service that week, with a much later more intimate one when her ashes would be interred. We decided to stay south rather than returning home knowing we could join her family for the later service. I wrote a note of condolence and memories to send with my daughter who would attend the first service.

Now this had not been the first death I had experienced. By then I had mourned grandparents, parents, in-laws and other friends. I was surprised at how painful this particular death was. The friend had been a co-worker for many years when we job shared before anyone had described that concept. We played bridge in a group and attended Community Concerts together, long before our hair was blue enough to fit with the audience. She was a marvellous cook and a dinner invitation to her home was a blessing. Our kids matched hers fairly well in age and had become good friends.

However, after we moved from the Hamilton area our contact was much less frequent. We no longer job shared nor played bridge together. She had become much less present in my life. We could go months without meeting yet the news of her death was much more painful than I could have anticipated.

I am a passionate, perhaps obsessive reader. One day while reading a book by Anna Quindlen I found this phrase "the worst thing about losing a friend is that you lose the part of your life you shared with that person." I don't think I had ever seen this explained so clearly and it identified to me why my grief was so intense. No one else could remember the day we were awed by a Spanish tenor singing entirely in Italian. No one else could remind me of an interesting patient whose treatment we shared. No one else could understand the grief we felt when our mentor/employer died.

Despite the other losses I think that was the first time that I truly recognized how sad it was to lose someone to whom you could say "do you remember the time that we.....?"

From that came the realization that as I grew older enjoying my good health, some friends and family would not. I hadn't known until then that the price I was to pay for living longer was the loss of so many people who had enriched my life. That became the surprising bitter that went with the better of longevity.

This was the start of the surprises that have been occurring to me as I add years. That's the point when the "nobody told me" thinking began.

Nobody told me the price I would pay for my long life was the ongoing loss of family and friends.

You're Never Old Enough to be an Orphan

It is wonderful to know your grandparents, to have your parents live into your own adulthood. Such a gift it is to be able to hear stories, not just of your own childhood but also of those in the family before you. There is comfort in an extended family. It feels like an imaginary but real roof over your head, all those people with whom you share DNA. The family cocoons us.

Stories are told of your early life and their early lives. We learn how Grandma made her great butter tarts or how Dad could always get a balky lawn mower to run. We are told about our earlier years, reminded about family characteristics and oddities, taught the bases of much of our adult decision-making and how we view the rest of the world. That sense of history is a comfort. There are always questions to ask, and sometimes we don't know those questions until we are well into adulthood.

I remember my father saying when his mother died (his father having died ten years earlier) that he was now the top generation. I never fully understood his remark until my mother followed my father in death. I did not know how lonesome it would feel to be the top generation. I did not know how many questions I still had that I should have asked. I did not know how much I still wanted their wisdom, their stories, their reassurance and their comforting presence in my life.

Nobody told me you are never old enough to be an orphan.

About Dodie

I am nearing 80, in pretty good health. My hair is almost white, I have dangling stuff under my arms, the creases and wrinkles on my face grow deeper and I'm usually in bed by 10 pm.

I take only one prescription medication daily. My knees are now both made of titanium. They do set off the airport warning signals, but I can walk into the airplane, survive a long flight and then walk for hours on cobblestones. I can walk briskly, squat to pick up a golf ball and dig in the garden. In short, they work.

However, and this is the big one. The losses in my life continue, both family and friends. With each death I lose that little piece of myself that I shared with them.

I have just finished writing a farewell note to my college roommate. Her husband phoned me two nights ago to give me an early warning, as it were. She lives in British Columbia and I in Ontario so a quick visit to her bedside isn't possible. Her leukemia which had been declared gone last summer has returned like a fiend and is causing her body functions to shut down, one by one.

We have known each other for over 60 years. We met in strange circumstances, roomed together for a year and a half at university and became good friends despite our differences. We maintained that friendship with frequent physical contacts before she moved west. Since then there have been visits, with travel in both directions.

This past summer we spent three sweet days at her home, talking too much, visiting the Okanagan wineries and eating well. At that time she was well, happy, active and seemingly rid of all disease. The times between visits we would e-mail and phone, sometimes with long intervals between contact, being able to pick up the relationship as if we were still living together daily.

These two days have been full of memories of the events we shared, the changes in our lives and once again the realization that I will not be able to ever again say to her "do you remember the time…?"

Nobody told me how much I already miss her.

The Importance of a Chance to Mourn

As I began to review many of these brief thoughts I realized how many of them deal with death and dying. This may seem like morbid focussing on that subject but one of the realities of aging is that there are more funerals and fewer weddings or baby showers on your calendar. Nobody told me how glad I would be to get an invitation to a gathering that wasn't a celebration of the life of someone I cared about.

I also have learned how terribly important it is to have a public time to speak of the deceased. As a young person when I attended a funeral I would feel foolish uttering the words I'm so sorry, thinking how puny my sorrow was in relation to the sorrow of the wife, husband or child to whom I was speaking. I also remember as a 13 year old the shock I felt when I heard laughter at the informal visiting time after the service. At that age I felt it was incredibly inappropriate.

I think my first recognition of the healing power of public mourning was my at father's service. Many people came to me, sharing stories of their time with him, often long before my birth, telling me of his youth and of his life beyond our family. They broadened my knowledge of him as a man in a wider community. I knew him as my father; they knew him as a friend, a work colleague, and an athlete. They told stories and I was able to laugh at some of them. The laughter was healing and the stories comforting to me. I learned then how important it was for me when they shared the admiration and affection they had for him. I also started to learn how important it was for them to deal with their own sense of loss by sharing those things.

Several friends and family have chosen over the years to avoid having a funeral or celebration of life of their deceased relative. Those family and friends have deprived themselves of the comfort offered by others who grieved. This avoidance also deprived the others who cared a chance to share stories and speak of their own feeling of loss. Most recently I heard of the request that when the ashes of the deceased were being placed in the family plot no one was to be allowed to say anything. I picture the mouths of the assembled family covered in duct tape to ensure their silence.

I find that when a decision is made for no service of remembrance I feel cheated. I want to have an opportunity to say how much that particular person meant to me, how much I cared. I want to share their contributions to my life and to the larger community, to add to the validation of that person's life. I want to comfort the family with those thoughts.

Both my husband and I have asked our children to organize a good party, with an abundance of food and wine served in a comfortable setting when we die. Because, I know now what I didn't those many years ago, it is important to offer the ones who care a chance to share their feelings and memories.

Nobody told me the service of remembrance is for all those who care.

Grief is love with no place to go.

Jamie Anderson

Being an Only Child is not all it's Cracked up to Be

I guess technically I'm not an only child, but it certainly feels like it now. I am the youngest of three children – born after two brothers. That's a good place to be in the birth order; you get to see what your older siblings do that works and what they do that doesn't. A girl with older brothers also has an advantage once she gets into the real world. Although they were my protectors against outside bullies, they did indeed push me around both physically and emotionally. I learned good defences early and rarely feel intimidated now, but there certainly were days when I thought how nice it would be as an only child.

My eldest brother, six years my senior, died two years ago after undergoing two below knee amputations because of diabetes. He was very clever in his work as a chemical engineer, always hungry to know why and how things happened. He used this research ability to investigate health resources and sometimes out thought his physicians. I believe he managed to delude himself that he could control his diabetes through diet and weight control. Sadly he lost that control, lost two lower legs and then his life.

The six years between us was huge in my early years but the gap seemed much less as we grew older and we became close despite the physical distance between us. We were both children of the sun. I would phone him at the winter equinox, as the earth begins its tilt to longer days, reminding him the darkest days were gone. We were also somewhat fanatical about maps, rushing separately into a welcome centre when we travelled together so we each could have our own copy of the local map.

After he graduated from the University of Toronto (UofT) he worked in a paper mill in northern Quebec. He then moved to the west coast, working in various pulp mills and eventually doing major consulting for mills in the Far East. We went west to visit many times, first to Vancouver, then to Vancouver Island and then after his retirement to Hornby Island. Conversations were never dull as we debated local, regional and world news. He was involved in various projects on a volunteer basis on the island, dealing with the limited water supply, plans for a cable ferry system and was instrumental in the building of a medical clinic for the island residents.

A visit to him would always include a hike through a west coast forest, with lessons on flora and fauna. My visit after his first amputation was particularly sad because there was no walk through anything wilder than the grass and gardens surrounding his house.

My other brother, not quite 2 years older shared more of my childhood with me. We were just a year apart in school and especially during our high school years were involved in many shared activities including the concert band. To his dismay we were sometimes thought of as twins. He began at UofT the year before I did and volunteered my services to head the make-up crew for the engineering faculty revue, Skule Nite, in my first year there. That was an interesting and challenging introduction to university life, but was great fun and a learning experience in ordering supplies and managing volunteers. One of the big challenges was pretending that I knew enough about makeup art to make someone look like Ed Sullivan!

My course was a three-year diploma in Physical and Occupational Therapy, his a four year Honours program in Mining Engineering. I had, in good little sister fashion, teased him forever that I would graduate before he did. I did manage that only because my graduation was held one day before his.

He went on to earn his MBA and worked for the Ford Motor Company for many of his years. He and his wife travelled widely to many exotic locations, returning with stories of foreign lands. He suffered a stroke this past fall, and worked very hard to regain his mobility. I remember a visit as he worked on his handwriting so he could sign his application for a drivers' licence renewal after his 82nd birthday. He was able to renew his licence but changed his mode of transport to a wheeled walker. He sent us a picture of it describing all its many advantages in a way that would have made the Ford advertising team proud.

He died six months after the stroke with a massive heart attack at home just as he was achieving some physical independence again.

So, although I was once one of three I feel now that I am an only child. There is no one alive who knew me when I was three, or seven or eleven - who can answer when I say "do you remember.....?" Those who have always been only children may well answer, "so what". I guess you can't miss what you didn't have, but I was gifted with two brothers and now have neither. I am now the oldest and the only one of my family.

Nobody told me how little I wanted to be an only child.

Mourning a Garden

Sensibly, we moved several years ago from a 2 storey house, with 4 bedrooms, 3 bathrooms, living room, family room, rec room on a wide, deep lot with an in ground pool. Living there were we two adults, in our mid 70's and a German Shepherd who was also ageing.

It was far too much house and yard, although it had been wonderful for 35 years. There had been room there for kids and grandkids. We hosted track team pool parties, the whole gang at a Visites Interprovinciale one fall and about 35 oarsmen from Club Espana one Henley regatta. When the kids gradually left we had room to house visiting friends and relatives, out of town family, school friends and visiting rowers during Henley week.

From that big house we moved to a bungalow town house in a nice area, lots of activities in the clubhouse and neighbours with similar interests and activity levels. The move was so sensible. The townhouse has all the living area on one floor, a loft for sewing and office space, lots of storage and tiny garden areas at the front and back. My husband delights in watching someone else remove the snow and cut the grass.

The sadness I felt thinking of the garden I left behind surprised me. The first spring, two weeks after our late March move, I wept on my way from Niagara Falls to Vineland as I looked at daffodils and fruit blossoms picturing what my old yard would look like.

It's hard to cover the traces that tears leave. I felt so foolish explaining to my husband that I was mourning my garden. I had about 30 different varieties of hostas but had room here for only three. I had been growing rhododendrons for 25 years and left deep red ones that were 7 feet tall and covered in bloom every spring. There was one creamy white one, with deeper colour centres that reminded me of the cream we used to steal off the top of un-homogenized milk. You know the cream in that little bulbous glass at the top of the milk bottle. The blooms of that rhodo were almost a foot across.

The second spring I found that I was still mourning the garden. I remembered the pleasure it was in past years to walk through the garden daily as the snow receded and the frost came out of the ground wondering if all my favourite perennials had survived. There were little yellow specie croci right up against the concrete front porch, which faced south. They would sometimes bloom the first week in February stealing two weeks on all the others because of the heat trapped there.

I would watch the Juncos snack on the later yellow and purple croci, enjoying what must have seemed a salad bar after a winter of dry seeds. Our yard had once been part of a sweet cherry orchard. One big old tree that had survived would spread its glorious white blooms, and the purple finches would bite at the base of the blooms and make a snowstorm of petals.

I planted daffodils in clumps of 5 or 10, which would grow into clumps of 20 or 30. Everywhere in the yard there were daffs of slightly different varieties and heights, which spread out the glow over three or more weeks.

Tulips were more difficult as the squirrels regarded them as theirs not mine. I had a few irises, special ones including a pure sky blue. Clematis grew on trellises and fences, deep blue Jackamani, two-tone mauve/purple and a red that was like velvet. There were purple, white, bi-colour and reddish violets growing everywhere as ground cover, sweet woodruff which is even sweeter than its name implies, and forget-me-not that self seeded everywhere. I loved the pale blue cloud over the ground that paired so well with the early bulbs. The sweetness of the woodruff had to compete with a double white French hybrid lilac, brought from our home in Hamilton 35 years before.

Then the rhodos and azaleas would bloom, surprising with their wealth of bloom and colour. Shasta daisies everywhere were hard to contain and control but cheerful and great for bouquets on a patio table. And I had daylilies – the wonderful ever-blooming Stella d'oro, its yellow and red offspring hybrids and Little Business, the pink one. They multiply and bloom almost constantly. There were other lilies, the orange and yellow "ditch lilies" that grow wild everywhere in Ontario, and their fancier cousins in a multitude of colours and combinations. I fell in love with Asiatic lilies and they thrived in the shade, soil and climate of that yard.

I had a collection of carpet roses, the first ones purchased at what then seemed a terribly high price of $25 each. They would bloom with the first daylilies and continue until a very hard frost stopped them. The magnolia we planted 15 years before we moved would stop traffic, and we left a small bit of grass in the front yard so the petals could scatter over it as they fell. A dogwood planted at the same time would astonish yearly as it raised its white bracts to heaven.

I have four small rhodos and one Japanese tree peony that I transplanted to this garden and seem not to have killed. I speak to it gently and ask it to be safe. There are a few hostas, not the best of my collection and in April the little bulbs are coming up – croci, mini daffs, schilli and species tulips. I brought lungwort for its blue turning pink spring flowers and its ongoing spotted leaves.

I must think carefully when I go to a garden centre now, as space is so very limited. I have taken over some fallow ground under a big old pine and this year my neighbour has asked me to extend the garden to the area under his pines. The new area means I can have more fun at the garden centre. I knew that I would miss the garden, although not the heavy spring and fall clean-up work. Still I cried for that garden the first spring and the second one as well.

Nobody told me that I would mourn a garden.

> *A garden is always a series of losses set against a few triumphs – like life itself.*
>
> *Mary Sarton*

Food can Say I Love You

I read with some astonishment about some new condo apartments being built without a kitchen. There are several reasons stated for this surprising change such as millenials being too busy to cook and takeout food and/or delivery being easily available services. One of the most plausible is that omitting a kitchen can reduce both the square footage and the cost of the apartment by a huge amount. Interesting to hear that kitchens are out, when even single rooms or suites in retirement residences usually have a small area with a stove, microwave, simple fridge and a few cupboards.

Cooking real food at home is good for so many reasons. It can be both economical and healthy, as all the ingredients are known and controlled. Cooking at home then sharing that meal with family or friends creates bonds. Making an old family recipe to honour the past, serving birthday cake on the special pedestal plate or sharing a recipe that the newest member of the family brings from their past all help cement family relationships. Cooking can also be an act of love. My husband knows that when I am serving macaroni and cheese with a cabbage salad on the side I am actually saying I love you.

My daughter gathered recipes from everyone in the family about 20 years ago and compiled a Cline Family Cookbook. There are many tried and true old friends in the book as well as nice ones that were new to me because they came from the in-laws. I still use that book, have added to it and know how to look for the stained recipes when I can't think what to make for dinner tonight.

Nobody told me how much love I would be serving every time I made a meal.

Cooking is like love – it should be entered into with abandon, or not at all

Harriet Van Horne

Cooking gets More and More Interesting

Cooking is an act of creation just as quilting and painting are. The good part is that the satisfaction and the fun of creation are there. The other good part is, if the recipe is a failure or the family (even the dog) reject it, the food isn't expected to last and be admired forever.

We are blessed in Canada to have a continuing stream of immigrants from all over the world. Each new wave brings with it new recipes, new foods, new spices and new tastes. Many immigrants have come because of want in their home country and have learned how to cook satisfying and healthy food from much simpler ingredients than North America has traditionally used.

In my grandparents time meals were basic meat and vegetables, with usually a sweet baked dessert to follow. Spices were limited and sauces were usually either gravy made from the roasted meat or a simple white sauce for puddings or vegetables.

Recipes from poorer traditions use far less meat, often combining two or more carbohydrates to form complex amino acids, which we get from animal sources. The traditional rice and beans of Caribbean cuisine is an example. Many of our immigrants have come from much hotter countries. I sometimes wonder if the elaborate spicing that accompanies those cuisines was to cover the possibly not quite fresh ingredients.

Whatever the reason, we now have access to ingredients our grandmothers had never heard of. There are hundreds of cookbooks featuring different country's foods and a recipe on line for almost everything. Using simple ingredients, stretching out the expensive meat proteins with tasty additions or avoiding them altogether with combinations of foods means we can cook well and save money along with it. I love finding out a new way of cooking a favourite meat, finding a new vegetable and playing with all the wondrous spices and sauces I find in almost every Canadian grocery store.

I am cooking more economically and much more interestingly these days.

Nobody told me how many ways there were to make excellent and healthy food.

My Love/Hate Relationship with a Dishwasher

Many years ago, in our first house we had just a little more than $4 left over each month after fixed expenses. I define fixed expenses as the cost of things essential to survival, which certainly does not include meals out or exotic vacations.

I do love reading those columns in the business pages of newspapers talking about how to budget. For many people, especially in the early years of marriage, home ownership and parenting, the suggested categories seem unrealistic and often funny. Even now, in our retirement years we really don't budget a certain dollar amount each month for clothing or for dining out. We don't spend enough each month on either of those categories to make it worth the column. It seems unlikely that these items are part of essential spending, until you discover that your last pair of underwear just lost all elasticity.

In the early years the budget covered mortgage payments, taxes and insurance. It included car insurance and gas, with a prayer that nothing serious would happen to the car that year. The amount budgeted for food also covered exciting items like toothpaste and toilet paper, laundry soap and shampoo. The $4 in excess was what I referred to in the first paragraph.

Things got easier and there was actually money that could be used to make discretionary purchases. My husband offered to purchase an automatic dishwasher but I felt it was a huge extravagance since hand washing dishes worked and it was a sociable activity. I said no and then no again and eventually yes. That was of course several years after the $4 left at the end of each month had grown sizably.

The argument that eventually won me over, after I had worked and reworked our financial status several times, was my husband saying it seemed wrong that such an attractive woman should spend her time washing dishes.

I suppose the other solution was for him to take over the job, but his argument was too appealing to resist.

So we went shopping, bought a really good dishwasher at a really good price and had it installed. I loved the fact, especially during summer months, when everyone in the family had a glass of something or a snack hourly that storing all those dirty dishes in the machine kept the counters clear and tidy. I did miss the opportunities to share news of the day with whoever got picked to help with dishes that night. Working or walking side by side makes for easy chatting since face-to-face conversations are more likely to be confrontational and less satisfactory.

I grew to love the ease of this machine. It made entertaining guests so much more fun as it worked while we lingered over coffee and dessert. That balanced out the loss of the camaraderie of catching up on gossip and girl talk while we jointly did dishes.

We moved and included space for a dishwasher in the newly designed house. It arrived the day we moved in and earned its keep. Again, I liked the tidy counters and missed the visiting over the clean-up task.

Thirty-five years went by and we moved again, this time to a somewhat tired townhouse with no dishwasher. There were many updates to be done, some cosmetic and some essential. The kitchen needed major upgrades. It took three years of living in the house and using the kitchen before we knew what changes we wanted. The kitchen was made wonderful and the upgrade included a dishwasher.

Today, when I loaded it with the flotsam and jetsam of two people who love to cook and eat, I patted it and said, "I think I finally have resolved our relationship. Today, I do love you".

Nobody told me you could love an appliance.

Cross-Stitched Irony

I called my mother's eldest brother Robert my Reverend Doctor Uncle Bob because he became an ordained United Church minister, then obtained Master's and Doctor's of Divinity degrees adding a diploma in Library Science in retirement. Despite his obvious devotion to study and education, he tried daily to balance cerebral tasks with physical tasks. He was a talented worker in wood, building a small table loom for my aunt.

Like him I like to use my hands and body daily in tasks that require physical skill. I have played with knitting and crocheting, sewing, painting, macramé and jewellery making. Except for gardening I tend to binge on a certain activity, before moving on to something new after a burst of creation in the first field.

Several years ago the cross-stitch bug bit me. I know starting with a simple 3" x 4" picture would have been sensible but that sounded so boring. I found a kit, with delightful Jacobean style flowers in two shades of blue. The finished project would measure 12" x 18". The flowers decorated the motto *Give me the grace to accept the things I cannot change, the Courage to change the things I can and Wisdom to know the difference.* I now know that it is called The Serenity Prayer.

I think early in my life I fought many windmills. The courage was there, it was the grace to accept and the wisdom to know the difference that was lacking. I hoped that stitching the words in cross-stitch, a slow but comforting process might help engrave them in my mind.

After the piece was finished, properly framed and hung I learned that it is a prayer that Alcoholics Anonymous uses in their program. It now hangs in my kitchen, visible to anyone seated in a specific chair in our dining room. As I offered wine to a guest recently the irony of the placement of the prayer struck me. I can understand fully why the words have meaning for someone trying to beat the hold that alcohol has on them.

I do hope that everyone also understands the meaning that these words have for all of us windmill tilters.

Nobody told me that this prayer refers to a very specific need for courage.

On Vision

Cataracts, the clouding and thickening of the lens of the eye is a slow process, causing losses that include decreased ability to see well after dark, loss of distance vision and changes in visual clarity as well as colour perception.

I have lived long enough to develop cataracts in both eyes and am lucky enough to live in a country where surgery to replace the clouded, thickened lenses with artificial lenses is available and successful.

Since the changes in my vision had been slow I was not aware of how much my vision had deteriorated, of how much clarity I had lost or of how dimmed colours had become.

After surgery on the first eye in summer, I remember my awe looking out into my garden at the intensity of the colours. The pictures I saw were clear, vivid and bright.

The colour truly astonished me. I think I drove my husband mad for the first two weeks reading signs to him, pointing out amazing flowers and spelling out every licence plate on every car we passed. What a joy to be given such clarity and colour back.

Nobody told me what a gift restoring good vision would be.

Which is Worse, to Lose Sight or Hearing

I am such a visual person that I have always felt that of my five senses, sight was the most important. Of course, hearing music is cool and touching a fabric or smelling a lilac in bloom are good, but seeing colour and reading are essential to my life.

I experienced a bizarre blocking of one ear several years ago. Apparently some strange virus or mould or something equally weird had invaded that ear and rendered me totally deaf on that side. My family physician irrigated the ear, without being able to clear it fully. I visited a specialist who literally vacuumed it to clear out whatever the stuff was. It was surprisingly awkward having my hearing diminished while I was having that treatment. I missed parts of conversations, had difficulty on the phone, as it was my phone ear and kept shaking my head in an attempt to clear it.

More recently a close friend, who had been deaf in his right ear since birth, suffered a sudden onset of total deafness in his left ear. He and his wife love to talk, spending hours planning and dreaming and remembering. He learned to lip read and they used a notepad, writing on it then passing it back and forth to communicate for complex things.

He gradually pulled into himself, avoiding most social occasions. His world, which had been full and busy, became small and insular. He was assessed and then approved for a cochlear implant. The process was long and complex, the surgery then the setup and fine-tuning of the device. The first time they visited us after this long process and we sat and talked, back and forth in near normal conversation. We were all in tears.

It made me realize how socially isolating losing hearing is and how important hearing is to our relationships.

Nobody told me that we truly need all our senses.

The Wonder of Engineers and Surgeons Recreating Human Joints

I have always been busy and active. Two of my nephews nicknamed me the Energizer Bunny, which I take as a fine compliment. As a kid climbing whatever height my brothers did, sliding down the same steep slopes, jumping from the same heights. I rode a bike, skated poorly, ran everywhere. As an adult I gardened and helped with every building project, lifting lumber and laying bricks.

I began to ski, first cross-country then downhill. On a trip to Hawaii I tried to surf and played in big waves. Both the skiing (or the falling while skiing) and the big waves did a nasty number on my knees, added to the already present wear and tear on the joint surfaces. I ended up with several small tears in the cartilages to add to the rough joint surfaces.

I met several orthopaedic surgeons who firstly cleaned up the cartilages, then later replaced the medial half of each knee joint until finally doing a total replacement of all the components in each knee. What a phenomenal thing this is.

To be able to remove the two halves of a joint, replace them with manmade bits designed and fitted for a specific person and have them actually work! Sure the recipient of the bits needs to work too, but the wonder of it is: I can walk and bend and lift and even run if I need to. The feeling of vulnerability when crossing a street is gone. I can move out of the way if I need to. My thanks go to the surgeons of course, but also to the biomedical engineers who figured out how to design these bits.

Nobody told me how awesome bionic knees would be.

The Importance of Light

Sunshine in the morning, candles on the table in November, a crystal vase set in a south facing window all light up my life. Every year I become more aware of how important light is to my mental well being. I read some words a long, long time ago. I can only remember the gist of the saying, not a proper quote. As closely as I can remember it says, you don't have to be depressed on the third gray day in a row, but it sure is easy.

My buffet and mantel hold clear, cut glass vessels. There are bowls and decanters, tall and short vases, candle sticks and candy dishes. They reflect and refract light which delights me daily. Sunshine on snow or late in the day when it intensifies the colours of flowers is the best of mood enhancers. I found a wonderful "trempe d"oeil" several years ago. It is a spiral of heavy wire with two faceted crystal balls enclosed, which hangs just outside of my sunroom window. When the wind blows the balls seem to roll down it and as they spin their facets cast rainbows across my window.

My elder brother, also a light lover, moved from Ontario to British Columbia because of his work as a process engineer in the pulp and paper business. He moved first to Port Alice, way north on Vancouver Island amid those tall, light stealing firs, then to Vancouver on the side of Mt Seymour, again in big tree land. His sojourn in Nanaimo on the shore of Georgia Sound was his only home in sunshine. After retirement he and his wife bought several acres on Hornby Island again part way up a mountain and in the middle of a typical west coast rain forest. Yearly he had to beat back the trees and undergrowth to let sun into his large garden and onto his decks. To add to the problem of those trees, Hornby is a long way north so winter days there are long. November can be a dreary month anywhere in Canada but on Hornby it is hugely so. Every year, on the day of the winter solstice I would phone him. The message always went – there did you feel the earth tip? For the next six months the days will get longer.

Meanwhile I continue to feed my need for light with my glass and my candles and try not to emulate a magpie too much as I feast on my shiny things.

Nobody told me that I need light like I need food and love.

Forever in Blue Jeans

There was a delightful song made popular by Neil Diamond in the 1970's called Forever in Blue Jeans. I realize that the lyrics were actually referring to a life style that meant wearing blue jeans forever as opposed to one where power suits and designer dresses defined you. I still enjoyed the thought of living forever in blue jeans.

Our three children ages ranged from 10 through 14 when I first heard it and they were, to a great extent always in blue jeans. Not always the trendy Levi ones but certainly blue denim. I saved the out grown and badly worn ones to patch the knees of the holey ones, because the 70's did not encourage the wearing of jeans with knees and other various lower body parts hanging out.

In the dark ages when I was in high school the only kids who wore blue jeans were male and often the techies, which then meant the ones studying practical matters like woodworking and electricity. A la Fonz, they ideally had enough leg length in the jeans to roll twice and still almost reach the ankles allowing a small glimpse of white crew socks.

Even in the mid 1950's when I went to University of Toronto girls wore skirts and I paired them in the winter with heavy weight ribbed knee socks that my mother had knit for me. Our classes were scattered across the campus and the winters were chilly.

I think I finally got some blue jeans in the late 1960's and discovered how useful and comfortable and sturdy they were. I continued wearing them and remember asking my husband when I should stop. His charming answer was "when you stop looking good in them." Since he has yet to tell me that I no longer look good I am still wearing them.

Just two days ago, on the day after my 82nd birthday I gladly put away all the dress slacks, skirts and fancy sweaters that I had been wearing over the Christmas holidays. I reached into the closet and pulled out my current favourite jeans, faded nicely from wearing and washing with back pockets decorated with gold embroidery and buttons and sighed that I will happily be, forever in blue jeans.

Nobody told me that Neil Diamond was right.

The Realities of an Aging Body

I don't know why I am surprised that the connective tissue in my body is losing its integrity. Or surprised that my skin is thinning while my jowls are thickening and my eyebrows begin to give me a distinctly Diefenbaker look. It really has nothing to do with denial of my age. I like being over 80. I've had so many good people and experiences in my life.

However, a quick morning glance in the mirror while I comb my hair often surprises me. The face is familiar, the white hair is not and often, for a fleeting instant, I see my mother or my elder brother looking back. Photos of me show an old woman with quite white hair (it was once almost black), wobbly upper arms, flab under the chin and everyone else in the family taller. I assume this is how I look to the world but it really isn't me. Everyone at a class reunion will have aged, except for me. I truly thought growing old would take longer.

Oh, and the last surprise, the hair that used to grow in my armpits now sprouts from my chin!

Nobody told me that all this would happen to me.

Beauty is the light, it's said in culture void of truth

Bury deep the fear of dead and strive instead for youth.

I prefer to set the stage with pride, my wrinkled face

And let my sleeve adorn my age with dignity and grace.

Quote from Wiley BC, by Mastroianni and Hart

Degrees of Separation

I've been reading up on the theory that anyone in the world is connected to any other person by only five others, explaining the phrase six degrees of separation. There are lots of experts who agree while many others say it's only true if you carefully sort out and research those five people.

I live in an area with a population of slightly under one million people. They are spread out through eleven relatively small towns and cities with a mega city of half a million

In this area if you cannot make a connection within two tries you just aren't trying, meaning (I think) three degrees of separation.

Nobody told me that six degrees could be a gross exaggeration.

Thoughts on Bucket Lists

I have just turned 80 which feels both surprising and good. I am living now in a community when 80 is more than the median age, but a long way from being a record. I have been asked to help celebrate 85th, 90th and 95th birthdays here.

People ask about bucket lists - do you have one, what's on it, are you crossing items off? I think I'm too busy just being busy to stop and make a bucket list. There are so many things I have seen and done that would never have been on a bucket list, if I'd thought to make one. So many good things happened because I volunteered for a job or committee, or I was lucky enough to be in the right place.

My mother overcame quite a bit of objections from the Girl Guide movement in Hamilton when she decided that there should be a Brownie pack on the Mountain where we lived. She made a convincing argument that she, an RN, could manage to be a good Brown Owl to some little girls who had no other organization to join. I continued into Girl Guides, earned my Gold Cord and volunteered as a leader of a company in Caledonia who were without a leader. I still thank my mother for introducing me to this wonderful movement.

In high school I helped to organize a musical weekend, arranging for billets for out of town choir, band and orchestra members. I learned how to do stage makeup and sewed costumes for actors in the Players Guild. I wrote for the annual yearbook and helped with a debating club.

In university I did make up for engineering revues, joined the university debates club and helped run a weekend of visiting debaters. I was on the council for my faculty, played touch football and helped organize an Open House at the HUTS (being the old army H-huts that housed the Physical and Occupational Therapy program.)

More volunteer opportunities came along; assisting with a girls Ringette league in Hamilton, helping start a league in St. Catharines, being part of the medical team and the weigh in crew at bonspiels and regattas, assisting with the High School Grape Olympics, being on the executive of my professional association and of a chapter of osteoporosis Canada, billeting overseas and local rowers for regattas, writing articles for the local newspaper, speaking about my profession and osteoporosis and gardening to community groups.

I was able to travel to several Canadian cities as a voting representative for my professional organization. My first real trip out of Canada was as team physiotherapist for a contingent from the St. Catharines Rowing Club to a regatta in Mexico City. Later, volunteering at regattas led to a chance to go to Europe as team physiotherapist for the Canadian Rowing Team in Lucerne, Switzerland and the next year to Duisberg, Germany. European travel was never on my "bucket list" but going as part of a national sports team, wearing a red and white uniform with Canada prominently displayed and entering the arena with the rowers as part of the team was an incredible experience.

I met many amazing people from several countries through involvement in rowing.

My mother had always kept a welcoming house and I learned early how to add the extra potatoes to the stew or Yorkshire pudding to the roast beef dinner when extra bodies showed up to eat. Saying yes to last minute guests was always fun. My husband and I have joined two travel clubs for seniors and have enjoyed hosting and being hosted by people from Canada, the US and Australia.

So at 80, I don't think I'll make a bucket list. So many interesting, satisfying and fun things have happened in my life up to this time. I think I'll just keep moving along, keeping an open house for old and new friends, an open heart for new experiences and watching for surprising things to happen.

Nobody told me that not making a bucket list was the best way to have a full life.

On Love and How it Changes

Nobody told me that the love you felt for your spouse on the day you married was a somewhat insignificant thing in comparison to the love you feel 60 years later. It is hard to even put them into some sort of scale to try to measure. Do you measure love by weight, by length, by volume, by strength, by drama?

It's good that what we call love at 21 is enough let us marry, to make those vows of "in sickness and in health, for better or worse as long as we both shall live." It begins with that first glow, that feeling that your life is incomplete without the other. Conversations are breathless and can take forever.

At 21 we feel immortal and strong and capable. We feel our love can handle any kind of challenge. Once what I would call the real world begins to assert itself, that feeling changes.

What was a place where only two people live becomes peopled with others, with their demands and their challenges.

Through the better times it is fairly easy to maintain and strengthen that love. Love being a dynamic and living thing, needs as a garden does, to be nourished and cherished. At the time we make those vows we have no idea how much our love will be tested through the worse times. The worse times can include conflicts in child rearing styles, a lost job, a move from a familiar city or pressures from other family. It can be the illness of a spouse. Not a cold or flu but the desperate, long lasting kind that means a loss of companionship and the comfort and pleasures of physical love.

In a good marriage love continues but it changes in subtle ways. There is still joy in being together, sharing our news, discussing world news and silly things like cabbages and kings. It is deeper, quieter and stronger in many ways.

Now after 60 years together we certainly still are in love, but it is a different kind of love. It's the glue of a shared past, the remembrance of shared jokes and triumphs, of holiday joys and holiday disasters. The many times to say, remember when. It is pride and pleasure in the accomplishments of the other and the wonderful quick understanding in a glance across the room. It is feeling like two people who are fully part of each other.

Nobody told me how much love changes over the years and how wonderful mature love would be.

You don't marry someone you can live with, you marry someone you can't live without.

Author Unknown

On Days That Grow Short

My husband and I just celebrated 60 years of marriage. The joke is: there were 56 good years and 4 not so good, the days making up those 4 years not all at once of course. A cross-stitch sampler made by a friend says Love, Honour and Negotiate, which nicely sums up a successful marriage strategy.

When we were approaching our 50th anniversary our plans were simple, our usual dinner out together somewhere nice and a not so serious discussion about making a commitment to one more year together. This had turned out to be a successful celebration for the previous 49 years and it had kept our marriage blooming through those years. We didn't feel that 50 years was such a big deal.

However our kids said 50 years is a big deal and needs a big celebration. So they planned an Open House, managing food from a fun caterer and their own capable hands, lots of drink, grandkids and great nephews to be servers and bartenders. Invitations were sent to family and friends and almost everyone came. It was a perfect day in May. The party happened in the house and in the garden and culminated in a big splash party, mostly the youngest generation, bouncing around on the heavy-duty pool cover. It was a fine celebration and it indeed was a big deal.

As the 60th anniversary came closer we talked for quite a while about what we would and could do to mark the date. Another big party seemed wrong, too many grandkids and great nephews and a great niece still finishing school or into a serious summer jobs relating to school. That was the first holdup – bringing family from Welland, Thunder Bay, Port Severn, Whitby, Toronto and Florida to join us in Vineland.

The second reason was more powerful. When we looked at the pictures from our 50th party there were so many missing from our lives 10 years later. Their absence would be keenly felt and would put a pall on the party.

The third seems to be summed up well in those fine words from September Song. "Oh the days dwindle down to a precious few, September, November….. and those few precious days I'll spend with you."

It seemed right and just that we should spend time together in this celebration together, just us. We chose two weeks in the Algarve, Portugal an area where we had never been. We walked, drank wine, toured wonderful old towns and enjoyed the sun and the Portuguese people we met.

So, as these days dwindle down we are together more, spend less time with our children and are trying to be a little less involved in volunteer jobs in our community.

Nobody told me how precious these golden days would be.

We may not have it all together,
But together we have it all

The Pleasures of Leaving the Snowbird Life

For the past few years we were part of the snowbird migrants who headed south leaving an Ontario winter behind. We never did four or five months away for various reasons. I delight in the changes of season in Canada and want to see friends, kids and grandkids. So for me, four or more months away from them and from home were just too many.

We travelled towing a trailer until 2012, going to parks mostly in Georgia until we realized how much warmer Florida was in February. Our medical travel plan offered unlimited number of 35 day trips, so we would go in November/December, come home over Christmas and then head out for February and part of March.

In 2013 we stopped at a park in the middle of Florida, in Lakeland. The city is small and delightful, full of many small lakes as the name suggests. The park was on the edge of the city, 6 minutes from Bealls and Lowes, 15 minutes to Publix. It had great recreation; three nine hole golf courses that were walkable, two pools, multiple shuffleboard courts, three recreation halls and great hiking trails.

We bought a non-mobile mobile home there as I couldn't or wouldn't drive what I called the train. By then we had a 29-foot trailer with a big slide and it was towed by an F150 with crew cab and midsized box. I didn't mind driving the truck but the two together were too much for me. The non-mobile home was a 35-foot, 30 plus year old trailer with a small attached Florida room on a pleasant lot. The price was reasonable with the Canadian dollar at par with the US then.

The trailer was adequate for the two of us. We did some minor renovations laying a stone patio with an overhead shade, removed some old, out of control plantings and made a new small garden. We repainted its weary exterior a lovely shade of lilac, with purple soffits. The annual lot rental was reasonable.

Moving to our current house and being away twice in the winter made summer travel less attractive so two years later we sold the travel trailer. It was fun heading down without a trailer, moving into our southern trailer which was already setup. We just needed to unload clothes, flip switches and open the windows before heading to Publix to stock the fridge.

We enjoyed our trips there but decided in 2018 to sell the trailer. There have been no regrets about the decision. It's the second week of February. The weather in December and January wasn't bad, just dreary. Our clubhouse is a 6-minute walk away with multiple daily activities and many friends. Happy Hour is weekly instead of almost daily, which is better for our livers. The house is warm with central heating. I have a freezer, dishwasher, washer and dryer and places to read, write, sew or crochet with a choice of two different cosy TV rooms so it doesn't really matter about the weather.

We are saving money. We are not golfing through the winter nor going out for lunch after golf. Food is cheaper because of the freezer, my big stock of basics and condiments and the ability and space to stock up on bargains. We no longer drive for 2 ½ days south and the same home, saving gas, motel and restaurant costs.

The most surprising thing is feeling as if someone just gave me back almost three months. Sure, I had those 70 days last year but I spent them driving, playing golf, idling and missing friends and family here. I participated in some events at the resort but being residents who were on an occasional basis pre supposed to less involvement. I do miss some of the people there and I miss being able to hike daily.

I have lots of volunteer things I do at home. I have begun a monthly book club, take part in organizing social events, chair the health and fitness committee and have just agreed to become vice president of a local club. Being away those 70 days interrupted most of those activities. So, this retired snowbird is at peace. I have more money, more time and many more interesting things to do.

Nobody told me how nice it would be to stay home in the winter.

Making Friends as We Age

To feel content in my life I need to have regular contact with people. Casual contacts with acquaintances and time with friends are both important.

However moving from acquaintance to friend is a process taking time and effort. There needs to be willingness to be open and honest, to share more than superficialities and to show both faith and trust. This was easy in our youth, a little slower and harder in middle age and significantly harder in old age. There can be a reluctance to make the effort needed to open up to a new person, to make that move from acquaintance to friend. This sadly can mean a decreasing circle of friends as those two monsters, death and dementia decimate our old friends.

Nobody told me I needed to work hard to combat lonesomeness as I aged.

How Liberating to Buy the Last One of Many Things

I have for many years done somewhat casual financial projections. There's never been anything as formal as a proper budget with categories for shampoo and toothpaste, clothing, subscriptions and all the usual utilities. I have always tried to keep a cushion for the big things such as replacing a roof or a car. In the last few years the projections have become much easier. Basically the projections are straightforward for known and fixed expenses. Those expenses sensibly include an amount for wine as well as groceries. We eat out on special nights but mainly eat at home cooking ourselves.

We're at the stage when we have moved to one car and it is likely the last one we buy. I remember buying a stove and a refrigerator and saying out loud that will be the last time we have to purchase those major appliances. I own three winter coats, which is more than I will ever need and two more than many people in this country have. One is a classy red wool that was my mother's, reserved now for special evenings, especially around Christmas. One is a puffy jacket, a gift from my daughter as my cosy thrift store buy bothered her somehow. The third is a sensible, warm, knock about kind of coat. I anticipate that they will all outlast me meaning I will never have to purchase a winter coat again. Just think of the savings.

The clothes that I purchase now are the boring things like underwear and socks, which do wear out. Shoes seem to last for a very long time and boots never need replacing. I don't need to buy new dishes, or cutlery or furniture or pictures to decorate my walls. There may be a wonderful new trend in dishes or cookware but my plain white dishes show off food so well and my stainless steel pots and cast iron casseroles will live forever.

When my orthopaedic surgeon explained all the pros and cons for total knee replacement, he included the thought that he would anticipate the knees lasting 20 to 25 years.

My husband and I looked at each other, smiling and saying, "Wow a lifetime guarantee."

Nobody told me that there would come a time when a purchase would be my last one.

On Memories of People we Loved

My very favourite first cousin's children recently honoured me by asking if I would deliver the eulogy at her memorial service. Preparing for this I recalled memories of things we did together, of her abilities, of her caring and of her amazing energy. I also called upon the childrens' memories. I spoke at length to her sister-in-law of many years and to a friend who was most truly her forever friend.

At the service the forever friend and I spoke of how devastating the loss of a friend of many years can be. I quoted Anna Quindlen's words that had given me so much comfort many years before. As we were talking I realize they weren't quite right. Anna spoke of losing the part of your life you shared with that person. You don't lose that part of your life, you don't lose the memories of those times.

The memories are still with you, but he/she is no longer there for you to say, "remember the time we....." So it is true that death deprives us of the person to speak to about those memories but the memories do remain with us to comfort in our loss.

Nobody told me I would keep learning the lessons of loss.

> *To live in the hearts of others is to never die in the love we leave behind.*
>
> *Carl Sagan*

Thoughts During a Pandemic

Today is part way through the eighth week of physical distancing due to COVID-19. I am reluctant to use the phrase social distancing, although that is part of what we are asked to do. I have crossed off so many items from my daily calendar – meetings, dance evenings, happy hours, dental and medical appointments, planning sessions, trips, meals out, teaching sessions and craft shows. The lack of deadlines is strange. I like an organized life and often feel that I am happiest when I feel as if I am balancing on a tightrope. I make daily to do lists and gleefully check items off when each task is done. This lack of structure is a bit unnerving.

The day starts later, morning coffee and newspaper reading takes longer despite the much thinner papers. Planning lunch and dinner seems to take longer as well. I had expected to do a lot of reading, more than my usual five to six books a week. Now I manage only one or two.

There is time for introspection and it has become a time of memories. As I paint a long neglected room in the basement it feels as if my Dad is with me, instructing me in proper techniques. He is smiling in satisfaction when I ensure that the brush I used is scrupulously clean so it can be used again.

We have been working on a 1000 piece puzzle since week one. It is done, except for about 100 pieces of sky – they are all blue, being light blue, lighter blue and very light blue. We may finish it, as it seems to have become a thing of honour. As I stop to work on it a bit, I am reminded of my older brother who would hide the box so that we couldn't refer to the picture and my other brother who always would pocket and hide one piece so that he could be the one to say "ta-da" as he tapped in that final piece.

I have been sewing, having the "F and F" mission described to me by a camping friend years ago. That stands for find and finish, which has meant 19 dresses for little girls out of slightly used pillowcases. I found a complex piece of cross-stitch more than half done and am working on it when the light is good enough. I am rehabilitating a worn and beautiful needlework cover for a fireplace bench, worked by my mother many years ago. The yarns have faded and in spots grown so thin that the backing shows through.

Because of this nasty virus and the age of my friends and neighbours here in our village that puts them in the most vulnerable category, I decided to make washable facemasks. At number 99 I ran out of both patience and elastic and stopped.

The virus has not touched us directly nor has it apparently sickened anyone in our village. It is scary but I think that those of us who lived through the Cold War in the 50's and events such as the Cuban Missile Crisis may be better able to manage the fear this pandemic is causing for some.

Perhaps this slowing down, this pause in my usual good, busy and satisfying life has been one of the better outcomes of this period. I feel as if I have learned that some things I do are important to me and mine, some are not and that sometimes, maybe even always, good enough is actually good enough.

Nobody told me how much I might like an empty calendar.

On Obituaries

I read obituaries. This may sound somewhat macabre but there are practical reasons. I have lived most of my years in two Southern Ontario cities being very involved in organizations in both. Because of my work as a physiotherapist I have many former clients. Reading the obits means that I am aware of local deaths and can react appropriately with expressions of sympathy and/or attendance at memorial services.

The less practical but more interesting, to me at least, is the window into lives that an obit provides. I find the ones that list only antecedents and descendants not particularly interesting. Obits that tell of immigration to Canada, the struggle to adapt and the eventual life well and comfortably lived are a pleasure to read. Some obits paint a full and colourful picture of the deceased. Occasionally the obit has been written in advance, by the deceased, which makes it even more interesting. The best ones combine both a true sense of the deceased and the love they gave and received in life.

One of my early thoughts as this pandemic began was that daily newspapers would begin to contain pages and pages of obits, which would be a continuing sorrow to see and read. The days when there are more than 2 or 3 pages are rare and often this dastardly virus is shown not to be the cause. What a nice surprise this has been.

Interestingly I have noticed a wonderful theme in many of the obits of women past 80. The obituaries are of women chiefly at home, lauded for cooking, baking and family gatherings. Of women who practiced the lovely skills of embroidery or quilting, who gardened, volunteered with church activities or ran community bake sales and organized charitable groups. The gardens they tended fed families and added beauty to their homes and neighbourhoods. These women were the force that held family and communities together.

I don't think that we will see such a cohort of talented, giving women again. Women have gained much by being involved in paid work outside the home. Our world has also gained as those talents are being employed in a larger sense, but we as a society have lost much of the glue that held communities together.

Nobody told me that a woman's role would change so rapidly in my lifetime.

Judy Cline

On Clearing Out and Ridding Up

We have been doing some serious cleaning of closets and cupboards during this stay at home time. We aren't total packrats but being in our 80's we have done our share of accumulating. Our next-door neighbours left their home of close to 20 years six months ago for a retirement home. This meant of course leaving behind kitchen contents, workshop tools, furniture, pictures and all the flotsam and jetsam of a long life.

We watched over the next few months as their out of country daughter and their out of town son came periodically to sort and clear out all of the furnishings. Some things, the most portable and cherished memory things went home with the children. Many went to our local charitable thrift shop and community service agency. By the time that ownership of the house was set to change, there were five visits made by a company whose job is to haul away and dispose of all the detritus of a household.

Watching this inspired us to do some weeding and disposing now so that our kids might only have to pay for one or two loads.

It has been both an easy and a difficult job. Some things that have been tucked away should have been gone months or years ago. Some things were important, much less so now. Our huge collection of records, both old 78's and many LPs are going. When restrictions lift they will be offered to one of several used record stores around. Some of them may even find a home that way.

Memories are surfacing of parents and siblings, of old friends and remembered vacations as we handle these items. We are also reminded of so many changes that have made our present lives so much easier. I remember my father getting up early to re-stoke our coal furnace and am grateful for the gas furnace and the thermostat on the wall that does all the work. I remember going on car trips with family and someone saying "did we turn off the water heater". If you hadn't, what the hot water tap delivered when you got home was chiefly steam.

As I open another box of facial tissues, I remember the "torn bockets" whose name came from out of nowhere in my memory. They were washed and ironed torn pieces of old sheets that we used as handkerchiefs at home. We used real cloth handkerchiefs when out of course. A bachelor great uncle would include a new and pretty hankie each year in a Christmas card to me. I still have two of these lovely things with scraps of lace around the edges.

As I wash our sealed double paned windows I remember the biannual putting up and taking down of storm windows that had been stored in the attic. I think I can still smell the Bon Ami paste that we used to clean them and remember standing looking through the window at a sibling to ensure the window was streak free.

I remember the cold cellar where there were carrots stored in a bushel of sand and you always picked the best apples, so even when they started to get soft you still had the best. I go to the grocery store now and buy fresh produce, brought in from all over the world anytime of the year.

I dust the wheeled tea wagon that was my mother's and remember having Sunday evening supper in the living room. It was always a light meal, because of course Sunday dinner was roast something at noon after church service. The memory comes back of listening to the radio show L for Lanky, with the theme song of "Coming in on a Wing and a Prayer." I assume now that Lanky referred to the Lancaster bomber, which now restored, makes flights from Hamilton around Niagara Falls in the summer.

I was speaking to my elder son a few weeks ago and telling him about these memories coming back to me. He told me, that between his bouts of raking grass and then shovelling snow he had also been recalling. As an aside, he lives in Thunder Bay so raking lawns and shovelling walks can both happen in spring. He says the memories weren't flashing but more crawling so he decided it had more to do with the current pace of his life rather than a warning about his imminent demise.

Nobody told me that tidying and sorting would be such a pleasant time of memory.

Entering Stage 2 of a Pandemic

The curve is flattening and in Canada, at the moment, we have fewer new cases, fewer deaths and a gradual but slow decrease in restrictions. Restaurants who since the middle of March could only offer takeout food are now allowed to provide service at outside patios. Some retail outlets have reopened. Strict distancing rules are in place, employees are masked and gloved. A clear screen usually protects those taking or handing out orders. Credit is preferred over cash and touchless terminals are available everywhere.

There seems to be a very slow response to some of the openings although the line-ups at a local outlet mall were apparently long. I can't imagine that all those waiting really needed a new pair of brand name shoes or a designer T-shirt. I'm guessing the need was more for a different experience than for an actual material thing.

Many of my friends and neighbours are remarking on the money they have saved during this prolonged semi-isolation. The sales of both groceries and alcohol have gone up hugely, which is not surprising considering that bars and restaurants were not open. We all saved on gas, as we had nowhere to go.

The downside of this is the many small businesses that have lost at least three months of revenue. Already there are closings in our area. Some may have been planned within a year or two but that plan was accelerated by the pandemic. Many businesses have morphed to provide very different goods and services. Locally we have wineries and a distillery that have turned their alcohol into hand sanitizing gels and equipment to sanitize cell phones and instruments instead of pleasant, tasty quaffs.

Here in the village we continue to walk, exchange e-mails, trade books and visit at a distance reluctant to get too close and perhaps undo all the good progress we have made to date. Cheers went up as hairdressers and barbers were allowed to open.

However, there is still no reason to do a proper house cleaning as inside visits are still not allowed. A neighbour claims she's not going to clean her house until she can invite guests for dinner.

Nobody told me the things we would miss most were haircuts and hugs.

Getting a Job At 82

A friend here in the village phoned me a few weeks ago to ask if I wanted a job. I really wasn't job hunting but her question intrigued me. Her son manages a plant in the next town that manufactures parts for hand dispensers. The parent company is over 40 years old, based in Europe and running full speed plus because of the demand caused by the current pandemic.

Most of the plant's operation is automated but the cylinders that go inside many of the dispensers are hand assembled, off shore before the pandemic, but in house now while they wait for an automatic assembler to be built and delivered.

Students had done the hand assembling over the summer but weren't available since return to school. I said I thought I could do a four-hour shift and agreed to work day on/day off with a friend. I didn't feel that this sometimes-achey body could manage doing it daily. Turns out

I was right. I am managing the every other day, with recovery time in between.

My decision was based on the need for help in a very important industry as well as a need to have some structure back in my life. It feels like old times when things got done because there were time constraints and dinner was planned the day before not at noon on the day of.

The job is of course totally repetitive and lacks intellectual stimulation, but it is quiet and cool, my co-workers are a similar age and conversation is good. The last line I worked on was in Weston's Bakery in Kitchener, where among other jobs I placed little boxes for butter tarts or scooped icing onto cakes on a conveyor belt. The pay was 60 cents an hour, with time and a half (90 cents) on holidays! This one pays much better.

Nobody told me I'd go back to work at 82.

I thought Growing Old would Take Longer

It has been so difficult through this pandemic period to truly believe that I am over 80. The residents of this village in which we live all qualify as the most at risk group for this particular virus. We have been in most instances a compliant group, maintaining proper distancing, avoiding group activities, eschewing coffee and TGIF gatherings. We're really good at hand washing because our generation was never allowed to sit down to a meal until our hands (and often faces and ears) had been inspected for cleanliness. The hardest thing for many of us has been to avoid the hug when there is a need to comfort.

So we are the vulnerable and at risk group. Many of us are very active, all live independently and for most our chief diagnosis is age rather than a mix of many diseases. Conversations on walks – talking across the width of the street – often include surprise at our age. We know what the calendar tells us, we know the date of our births but there is a strong sense of disbelief that we are now officially the elderly. We have coined a new term, "frelderly" for the most at risk because of age and frailty. Most of us only feel elderly!

Nobody told me that I truly would be old.

> *You don't look the way you feel and you don't feel the way you look.*
>
> *Pearl on Aging, Pickles*

The Physio becomes the Patient

It's late in December and I just turned 83. I am feeling sorry for myself, as I somehow set off a very hot, painful sciatica in my left leg. There seems to be no rhyme nor reason, nor any precipitating factor, which is confusing the physiotherapist in me. I even got to take my very first ride in an ambulance.

The EMTs were kind and friendly. However being on my back safely trussed, in a position that intensified the pain made me nauseous and I was grateful when the ride was over. The emergency staff got me onto a stretcher in a better position with lots of pillow props.

After a good assessment by the emergency doc, followed by lots of X-rays the diagnosis was an arthritic back (surprise, surprise at my then age of 82) with an irritated left sciatic nerve. I came home with heavy-duty anti-inflammatory meds and low dose morphine for pain.

I've received lots of good advice and helpful equipment from two physio friends and spent the days leading to Christmas doing not much except telling the two men in my life where things were in the kitchen and how long food needed to be cooked. The symptoms seem to be improving slowly, but it's been tough to be so restricted and so unable to fix myself.

Nobody told me how much harder it is to have the orthopaedic problem than to treat it.

The Ending to this Unusual Year

As we near the end of 2020, the year of COVID-19, we have made it through one more holiday so markedly different than in previous years. The summer gave us respite as we could gather safely outdoors and shout greetings to each other. Thanksgiving, Christmas and New Years forced major adaptations as we moved indoors and a second wave was predicted.

On the Saturday before Christmas we drove to Oakville on a dreary, damp day and met my Whitby daughter, her husband and their three sons in a park. We were all masked as we walked and talked for an hour then exchanged bins of gifts and sent non touching hugs to each other. It is the first year in 55 that we did not spend Christmas with our daughter.

My husband, son and I managed to make the traditional cinnamon buns to be formed Christmas Eve and baked early Christmas morning. The new part of the old was that Christmas morning we walked carefully through new snow to deliver small pans of warm buns to the neighbours. We should have been singing Good King Wenceslas while we did our deliveries.

We face timed, phoned and zoomed with family on Christmas Day. Not the same as being actually together but wonderful to see faces. Loving and thoughtful gifts were given and received and many, many "I love yous". Our daughters' most special gift to us was a framed saying – *Apart so we can be together again soon.*

I've always felt my birthday, which follows Christmas by two days, comes far too quickly for everyone's sake. We've just made it through Christmas and Boxing Day and when we really would like to go low key and suddenly it's Mom's birthday! This year the day was full of phone calls, Facebook wishes, wine and cookies at the door and the Plum Court ladies quartet singing Happy Birthday. So many friends - how they educate, warm and amuse me, enriching my life with their friendship and caring. So 2020 will be gone very, very soon. And quoting the Grinch – 2020 - stink, stank, and stunk. Begone!

Nobody told me the gift 2020 would give was the knowledge that all we really need are family and friends.

Afterword

The book has really happened. Big thanks go to friends here within Heritage Village: to Henry and Ernastine for their early encouragement and their cheerleading along the way, to Allen and Phyllis for their painstaking proofreading and fine editorial suggestions. Thanks to my Book Bunch (Eleanor and Phyllis, Carolyn and Marge, the two Pats and Sally) for their support and all the interesting books they find for us to read while we sip and nosh. All these people supported me through this writing experience and continue to broaden my world. Thanks go to my family who taught me so much as they grew and so did I.

Gentle readers (writers usually refer to their readers as gentle but who really knows if they are!) thank you for joining me. I hope that you also sip and nosh as you read about my journeying into the things I have discovered as I aged. I hope that they inspired your memories too and also maybe, just maybe, NOBODY told you these things either.

Finished on a bright February day in a Polar vortex and isolation still with us while the sunshine brings optimism for our future.

Judy Cline, Vineland, Ontario

www.ingramcontent.com/pod-product-compliance
Lightning Source LLC
Chambersburg PA
CBHW032036290426
44110CB00012B/827